# A SURVIVOR'S TALE

*art spiegelman*

PANTHEON BOOKS · NEW YORK

# FOR ANJA

Thanks to Ken and Flo Jacobs, Ernie Gehr, Paul Pavel, Louise Fili, and Steven Heller, whose appreciation and moral support have helped this book find its shape.

Thanks to Mala Spiegelman for her help in translating Polish books and documents, and for wanting *Maus* to happen.

And thanks to Françoise Mouly for her intelligence and integrity, for her editorial skills, and for her love.

Copyright © 1973, 1980, 1981, 1982, 1983, 1984, 1985, 1986 by Art Spiegelman.

All rights reserved under International and Pan-American Copyright Conventions.
Published in the United States by Pantheon Books, a division of Random House, Inc.,
New York, and simultaneously in Canada by Random House of Canada Limited, Toronto.

Chapters 1 through 6 first appeared, in somewhat different form, in *Raw* magazine between 1980 and 1985.

"Prisoner on the Hell Planet" originally appeared in *Short Order Comix #1*, 1973

Library of Congress Cataloging-in-Publication Data
Spiegelman, Art.
Maus: a survivor's tale.
1. Spiegelman, Vladek — Comic books, strips, etc.
2. Holocaust, Jewish (1939-1945) — Poland — Biography Comic books, strips, etc.
3. Holocaust survivors — United States — Biography — Comic books, strips, etc.
4. Spiegelman, Art — Comic books, strips, etc.
5. Children of the Holocaust survivors — United States — Biography — Comic books, strips, etc.
I. Title.
D810.J4S643   1986      940.53'15'03924024      86-42642
ISBN 0-394-74723-2

For more information about *Raw* magazine, write to Raw Books and Graphics,
27 Greene Street, New York, New York 10013.

Manufactured in U.S.A.

2468B97531

"The Jews are undoubtedly a race,

but they are not human."
Adolf Hitler

Rego Park, N.Y. c.1958

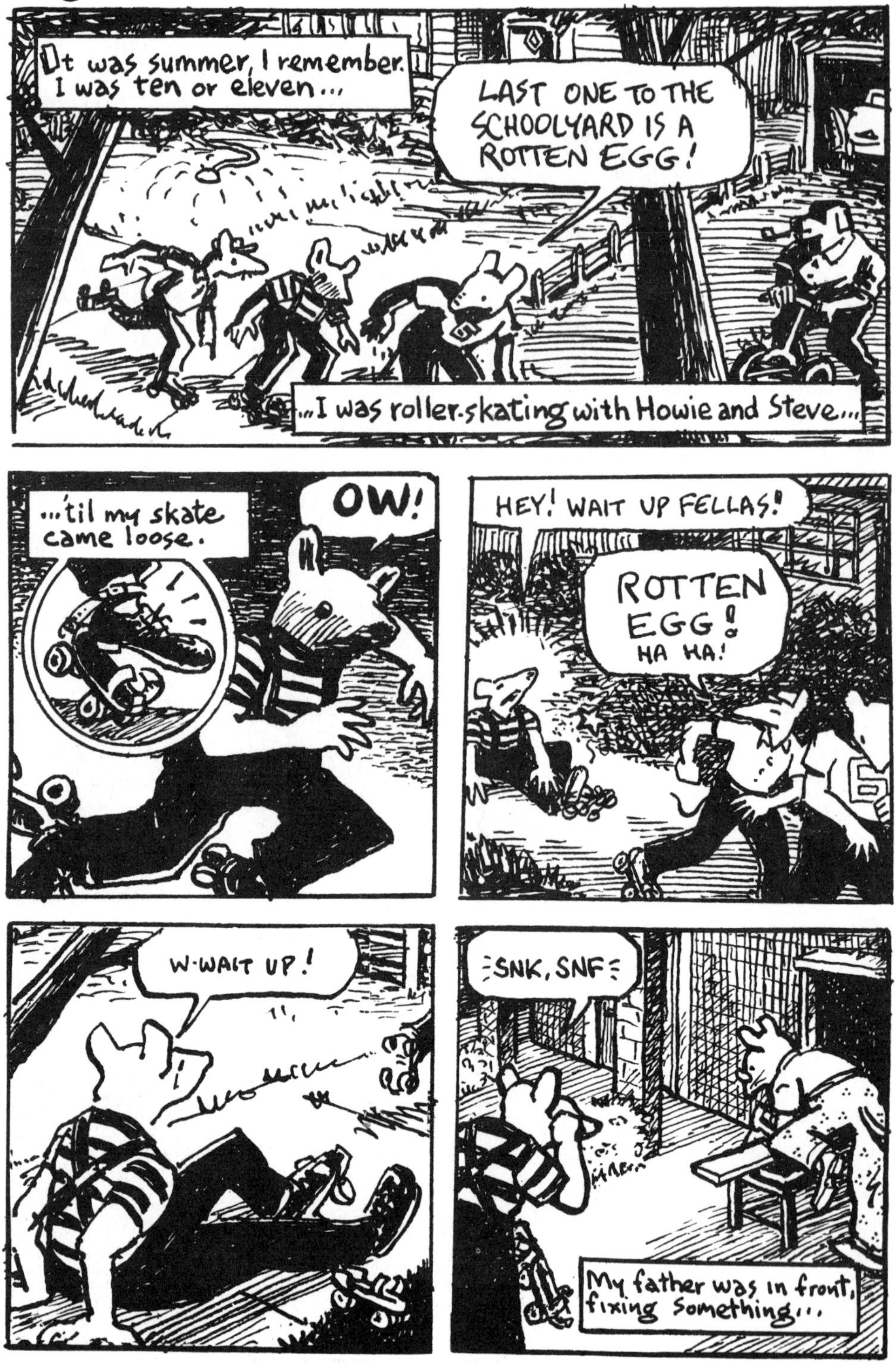
It was summer, I remember. I was ten or eleven...
LAST ONE TO THE SCHOOLYARD IS A ROTTEN EGG!
...I was roller-skating with Howie and Steve...
...til my skate came loose.
OW!
HEY! WAIT UP FELLAS!
ROTTEN EGG! HA HA!
W-WAIT UP!
SNK, SNF
My father was in front, fixing something...

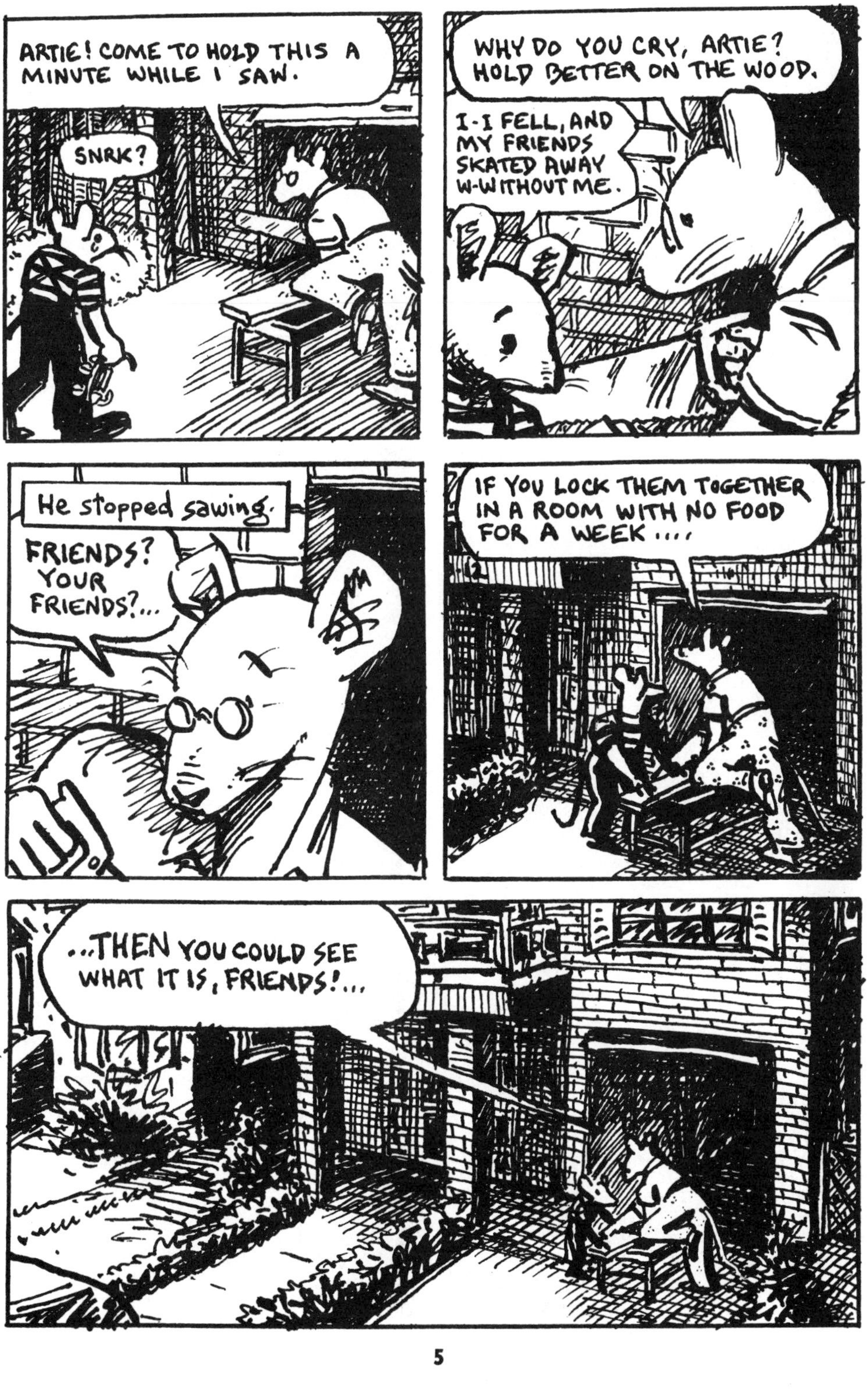
ARTIE! COME TO HOLD THIS A MINUTE WHILE I SAW.
SNRK?
WHY DO YOU CRY, ARTIE? HOLD BETTER ON THE WOOD.
I-I FELL, AND MY FRIENDS SKATED AWAY W-WITHOUT ME.
He stopped sawing.
FRIENDS? YOUR FRIENDS?...
IF YOU LOCK THEM TOGETHER IN A ROOM WITH NO FOOD FOR A WEEK....
...THEN YOU COULD SEE WHAT IT IS, FRIENDS!...

# MY FATHER BLEEDS HISTORY

## (MID-1930s TO WINTER 1944)

## CONTENTS

# CHAPTER ONE

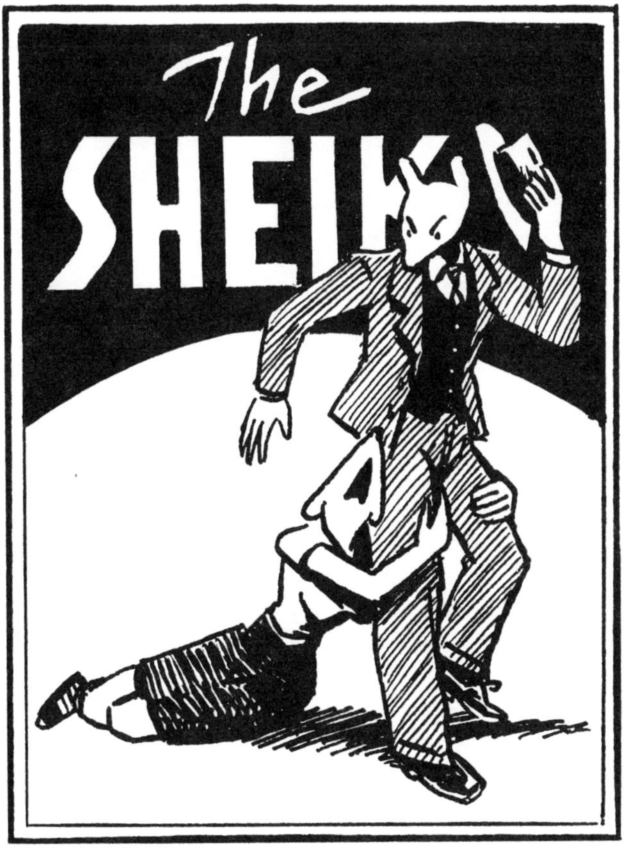
The
SHEIK

I went out to see my Father in Rego Park. I hadn't seen him in a long time— we weren't that close.

POPPA!

OI, ARTIE. YOU'RE LATE. I WAS WORRIED.

IT'S A SHAME FRANÇOISE ALSO DIDN'T COME.

UH-HUH. SHE SENDS REGARDS.

He had aged a lot since I saw him last. My Mother's suicide and his two heart attacks had taken their toll.

MALA! LOOK WHO'S HERE! ARTIE!

He was remarried. Mala knew my parents in Poland before the war.

She was a survivor too, like most of my parents' friends.

HI, ARTIE. LET ME TAKE YOUR COAT.

THE DINNER IS ON THE TABLE.

ACCH, MALA!

A WIRE HANGER YOU GIVE HIM! I HAVEN'T SEEN ARTIE IN ALMOST TWO YEARS— WE HAVE PLENTY WOODEN HANGERS.

They didn't get along.

After dinner he took me into my old room...

COME— WE'LL TALK WHILE I PEDAL...

IT'S GOOD FOR MY HEART, THE PEDALING. BUT, TELL ME, HOW IS IT BY YOU? HOW IS GOING THE COMICS BUSINESS?

I STILL WANT TO DRAW THAT BOOK ABOUT YOU...

THE ONE I USED TO TALK TO YOU ABOUT..

ABOUT YOUR LIFE IN POLAND, AND THE WAR.

IT WOULD TAKE **MANY** BOOKS, MY LIFE, AND NO ONE WANTS ANYWAY TO HEAR SUCH STORIES.

*I* WANT TO HEAR IT. START WITH MOM... TELL ME HOW YOU MET.

BETTER YOU SHOULD SPEND YOUR TIME TO MAKE DRAWINGS WHAT WILL BRING YOU SOME MONEY...

BUT, IF YOU WANT, I CAN TELL YOU... I LIVED THEN IN CZESTOCHOWA, A SMALL CITY NOT FAR FROM THE BORDER OF GERMANY...

I WAS IN TEXTILES—BUY-ING AND SELLING— I DIDN'T MAKE MUCH, BUT ALWAYS I COULD MAKE A *LIVING*.

I WAS, AT THAT TIME, YOUNG, AND REALLY A NICE, HANDSOME BOY.

I HAD A LOT OF GIRLS WHAT I DIDN'T EVEN *KNOW* THAT WOULD RUN AFTER ME.

RRING

HELLO, VLADEK? THIS IS YULEK...

A FRIEND OF MINE, LUCIA GREENBERG, WOULD LIKE TO BE INTRODUCED TO YOU.

THE SHEIK

PEOPLE ALWAYS TOLD ME I LOOKED JUST LIKE RUDOLPH VALENTINO.

PICTURE

EVENTUALLY, I TOOK LUCIA TO DANCE...

DO YOU LIVE ALONE?

YES.

I HAVE A SMALL APARTMENT. MY PARENTS MOVED TO SOSNOWIEC.

I'D LIKE TO SEE IT SOMETIME.

MAYBE SOMETIME.

WHEREVER I WENT - I LOOKED AROUND - AND LUCIA GREENBERG WOULD BE ALSO THERE ...

VLADEK! - WHICH WAY ARE YOU GOING?

JUST TO THE MARKET.

ME TOO - LET'S WALK TOGETHER.

BUT, POP... MOM'S NAME WAS ANNA ZYLBERBERG! ...

ALL THIS WAS *BEFORE* I MET ANJA - JUST LISTEN, YES?

WHY DON'T YOU EVER INVITE ME TO YOUR HOME? ... ARE YOU ASHAMED OF IT?

SHE KEPT INSISTING ME TO SHOW HER MY APARTMENT...

- SO FINALLY, I INVITED HER ...

EVERYTHING'S SO NEAT AND CLEAN!

I LIKE TO KEEP THINGS IN ORDER.

YOU MUST HAVE ANOTHER GIRL-FRIEND WHO CLEANS FOR YOU - NO?

NO.

... I DIDN'T WANT TO BE MORE CLOSER WITH HER, BUT SHE REALLY WOULDN'T LET ME GO.

14

WAS SHE THE FIRST GIRL YOU -UH-

YES...WE WERE MORE INVOLVED, SO LIKE THE YOUTHS HERE TODAY.

WE SAW EACH OTHER TOGETHER FOR MAYBE THREE OR FOUR YEARS.

LETS GET ENGAGED, VLADEK.

IT'S LATE. I'LL TAKE YOU HOME.

NOT YET, PLEASE

COME ON - YOUR PARENTS WOULD WORRY.

HER FAMILY WAS NICE, BUT HAD NO MONEY, EVEN FOR A DOWRY.

CZESTOCHOWA / SOSNOWIEC

DECEMBER 1935

WELL, EVERY HOLIDAY I WENT TO VISIT MY FAMILY.... IT WAS MAYBE A JOURNEY OF 35 OR 40 MILES.

COUSIN VLADEK!

IT'S GOOD TO SEE YOU AGAIN. LISTEN ....

THERE'S A GIRL IN MY CLASS-I WANT YOU TO MEET US TOMORROW - HER NAME IS ANJA.

SHE'S INCREDIBLY CLEVER, FROM A RICH FAMILY.... A VERY GOOD GIRL ....

15

THE NEXT MORNING WE ALL MET TOGETHER. MY COUSIN AND ANJA SPOKE SOMETIMES IN ENGLISH

HOW YOU LIKE HIM?

HE'S A HANDSOME BOY AND SEEMS VERY NICE.

THEY COULDN'T KNOW I UNDERSTOOD.

WELL- I PROMISED TO BE HOME EARLY... I'LL LEAVE YOU TWO ALONE

YOU KNOW, YOU SHOULD BE CAREFUL SPEAKING ENGLISH- A "STRANGER" COULD UNDERSTAND.

Y-YOU KNOW ENGLISH?

DID YOU STUDY IT IN SCHOOL?

I HAD TO QUIT SCHOOL AT ABOUT 14 TO WORK.

...BUT I TOOK PRIVATE LESSONS... I ALWAYS DREAMED OF GOING TO AMERICA.

IT'S A SHAME YOU HAVE TO RETURN TO CZESTOCHOWA SO SOON.

YES- BUT I HAVE MY BUSINESS.

HAVE YOU A PHONE AT HOME?

AS SOON I CAME BACK TO CZESTOCHOWA, SHE CALLED - ONCE A DAY.... TWICE... EVERY DAY. WE TALKED.

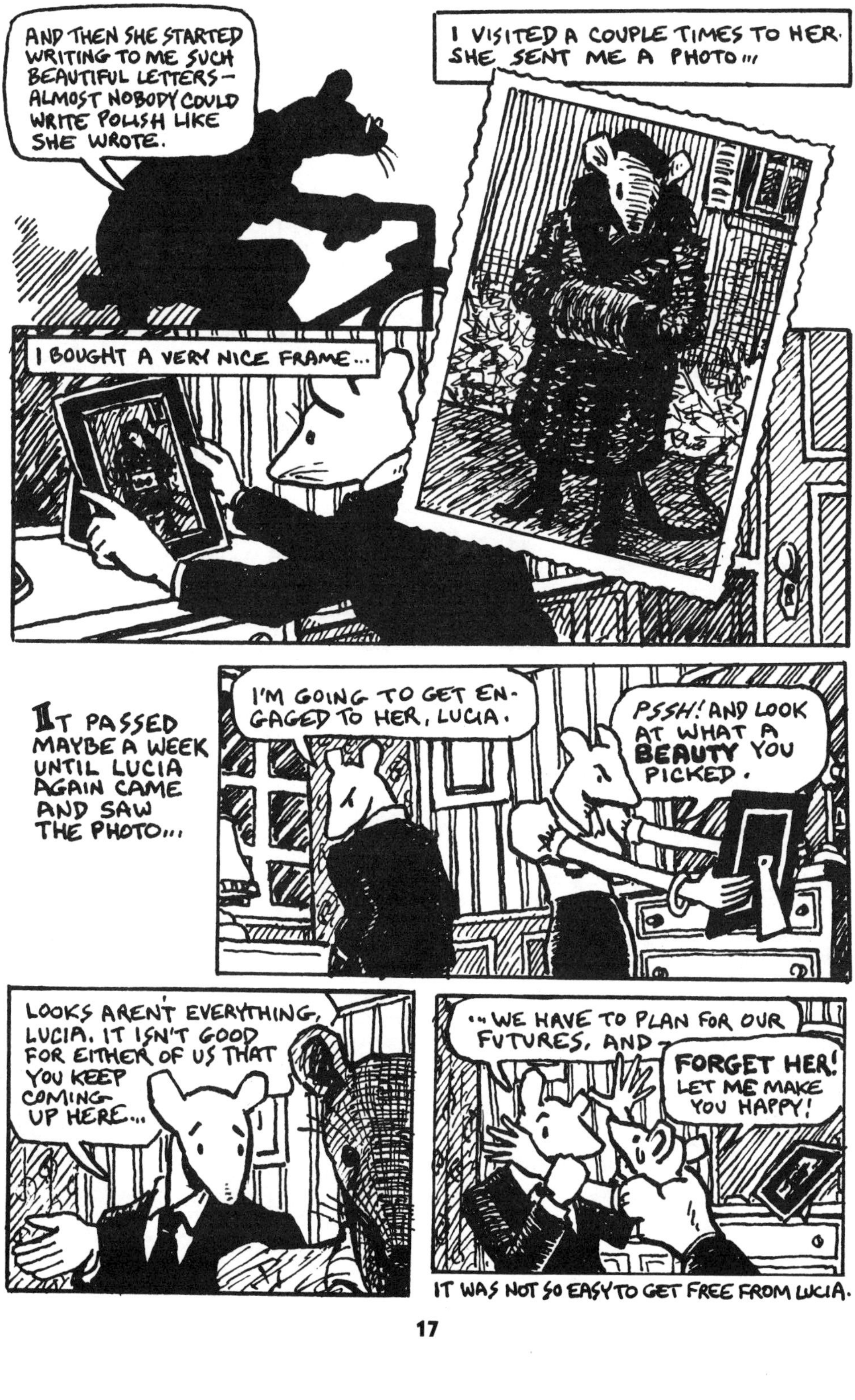
AND THEN SHE STARTED WRITING TO ME SUCH BEAUTIFUL LETTERS— ALMOST NOBODY COULD WRITE POLISH LIKE SHE WROTE.
I VISITED A COUPLE TIMES TO HER. SHE SENT ME A PHOTO...
I BOUGHT A VERY NICE FRAME...
IT PASSED MAYBE A WEEK UNTIL LUCIA AGAIN CAME AND SAW THE PHOTO...
I'M GOING TO GET ENGAGED TO HER, LUCIA.
PSSH! AND LOOK AT WHAT A BEAUTY YOU PICKED.
LOOKS AREN'T EVERYTHING, LUCIA. IT ISN'T GOOD FOR EITHER OF US THAT YOU KEEP COMING UP HERE...
...WE HAVE TO PLAN FOR OUR FUTURES, AND—
FORGET HER! LET ME MAKE YOU HAPPY!
IT WAS NOT SO EASY TO GET FREE FROM LUCIA.

MOM WASN'T THAT ATTRACTIVE, HUH?

NOT SO LIKE LUCIA... BUT IF YOU TALKED A LITTLE TO HER, YOU STARTED LOVING HER MORE AND MORE.

ONE TIME WE WALKED INTO THE DIRECTOR FROM HER SCHOOL...

YOU'RE VERY LUCKY, MR. SPIEGELMAN.

...YOU DON'T KNOW WHAT A GIRL YOU'RE GETTING—I'VE HAD MANY STUDENTS...

...BUT NEVER ONE AS SENSITIVE AND INTELLIGENT AS ANNA!

YES—THAT'S WHY I PICKED HER.

I WISH YOU COULD VISIT ME IN CZESTOCHOWA—I'D LIKE TO SHOW YOU OFF TO MY FRIENDS.

I'VE BEGGED MY MOTHER TO LET ME GO—BUT SHE'S SO RELIGIOUS AND OLD-FASHIONED.

...SHE WOULD NEVER ALLOW ME TO GO TO A BACHELOR'S APARTMENT!

ANJA'S PARENTS WERE ANXIOUS SHE SHOULD BE MARRIED. SHE WAS 24; I WAS THEN 30.

OH, MY PARENTS WOULD LIKE YOU TO COME TO DINNER TOMORROW NIGHT.

THE ZYLBERBERG FAMILY WAS VERY WELL OFF—MILLIONAIRES!

THE ZYLBERBERGS HAD A HOSIERY FACTORY—ONE OF THE BIGGEST IN POLAND... BUT WHEN I CAME IN TO THEIR HOUSE IT WAS SO LIKE A KING CAME...

WELCOME, WELCOME.

ANJA—VLADEK IS HERE!

MAKE YOURSELF COMFORTABLE WHILE I HELP WITH THE DINNER.

TO SEE WHAT A HOUSEKEEPER SHE WAS, I PEEKED INTO ANJA'S CLOSET.

EVERYTHING IS NEAT AND STRAIGHT JUST THE WAY I LIKE IT!

BUT WHAT'S THIS—PILLS?!

I WROTE DOWN EVERY PILL.

IF SHE WAS SICK, THEN WHAT DID I NEED IT FOR?

DINNER IS READY!

LATER, A FRIEND, A DRUGGIST, TOLD ME THE PILLS WERE ONLY BECAUSE SHE WAS SO SKINNY AND NERVOUS.

HOW ABOUT SOME MORE GEFILTE FISH, VLADEK?

SO, TO MAKE A LONG STORY SHORT, BY THE END OF 1936 WE WERE ENGAGED AND I MOVED FROM CZESTOCHOWA TO SOSNOWIEC.

ACH! HERE I FORGOT TO TELL SOMETHING FROM *BEFORE* I MOVED TO SOSNOWIEC BUT AFTER OUR ENGAGEMENT WAS MADE.

ONE EVENING THE BELL RANG ...

LUCIA

WHAT ARE YOU DOING HERE? I'M ON MY WAY OUT.

I-I'LL COME WITH YOU.

NO, YOU CAN'T COME WI-

PLEASE, VLADEK!

SHE FELL ON THE FLOOR AND HELD STRONG MY LEGS.

DON'T RUN AWAY!

I SAW NOW THAT I WENT TOO FAR WITH HER.

SLAM!

I RAN OUT TO MY FRIEND WHAT INTRO-DUCED US. HE WENT TO CALM HER DOWN AND TOOK HER HOME.

I DIDN'T HEAR MORE FROM LUCIA—BUT ALSO I STOPPED HEARING FROM ANJA...

NO TELEPHONE CALLS, NO LETTERS, *NOTHING!* WHAT HAPPENED?

HELLO, MRS. ZYLBERBERG. COULD I SPEAK TO ANJA?

SHE SAYS SHE WON'T SPEAK TO YOU!

BUT WHY?

SHE GOT A LETTER FROM SOMEONE IN CZESTOCHOWA. MY GOD! IT SAYS THE WORST THINGS IN THE WORLD ABOUT YOU!

WELL, I CAN'T CONVINCE HER ON THE PHONE. I'LL COME DOWN BY TRAIN ON FRIDAY AFTER WORK.

IT WASN'T EVEN A HOLIDAY, BUT I WENT ANYWAY TO SOSNOWIEC.

SO, TELL ME, ANJA—WHAT HAVE I DONE THAT'S SO HORRIBLE?

YOU SHOULD KNOW—JUST READ THIS!

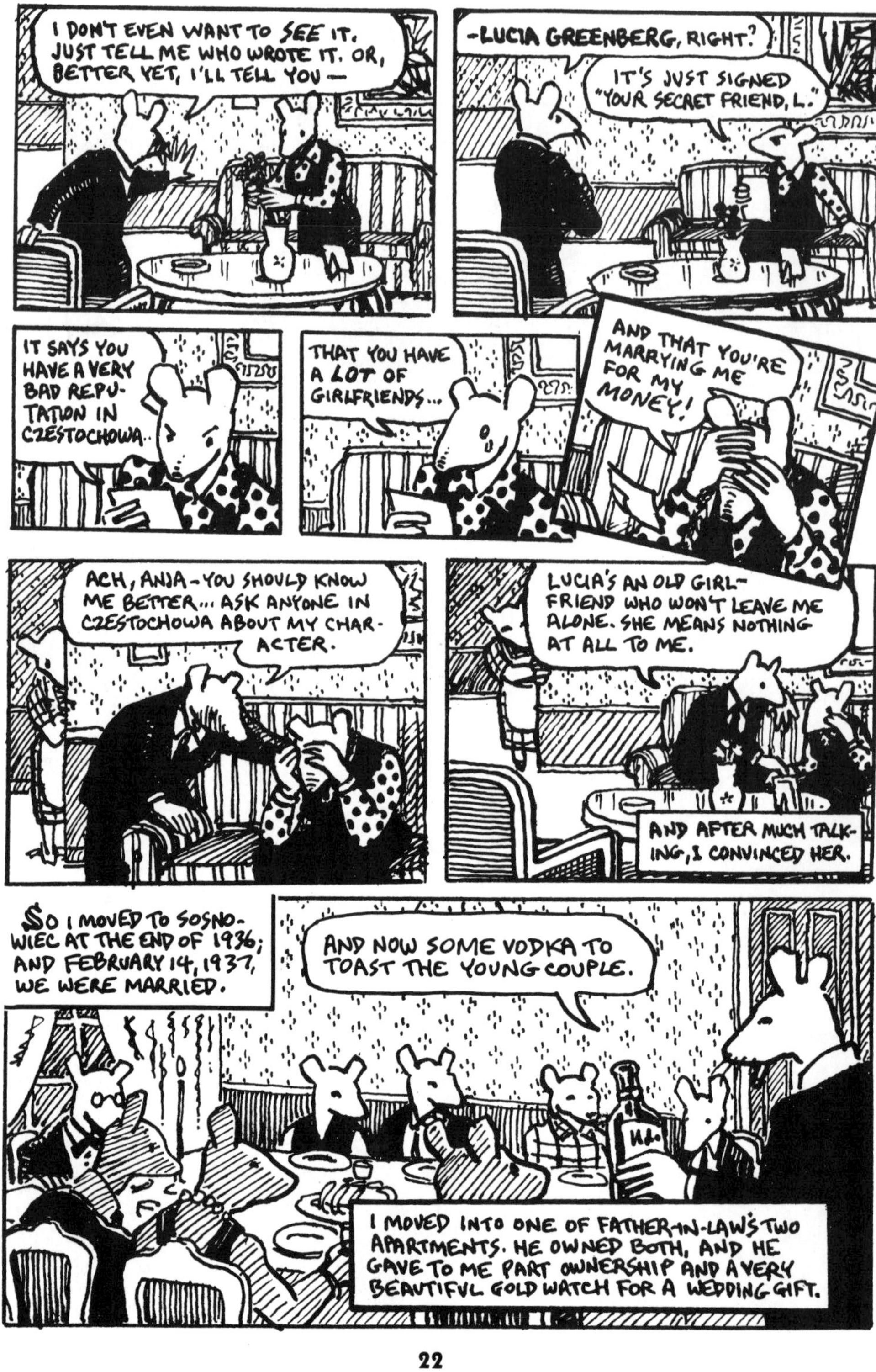
I DON'T EVEN WANT TO SEE IT. JUST TELL ME WHO WROTE IT. OR, BETTER YET, I'LL TELL YOU —
-LUCIA GREENBERG, RIGHT?
IT'S JUST SIGNED "YOUR SECRET FRIEND, L."
IT SAYS YOU HAVE A VERY BAD REPUTATION IN CZESTOCHOWA..
THAT YOU HAVE A LOT OF GIRLFRIENDS...
AND THAT YOU'RE MARRYING ME FOR MY MONEY!
ACH, ANJA - YOU SHOULD KNOW ME BETTER... ASK ANYONE IN CZESTOCHOWA ABOUT MY CHARACTER.
LUCIA'S AN OLD GIRLFRIEND WHO WON'T LEAVE ME ALONE. SHE MEANS NOTHING AT ALL TO ME.
AND AFTER MUCH TALKING, I CONVINCED HER.
SO I MOVED TO SOSNOWIEC AT THE END OF 1936; AND FEBRUARY 14, 1937, WE WERE MARRIED.
AND NOW SOME VODKA TO TOAST THE YOUNG COUPLE.
I MOVED INTO ONE OF FATHER-IN-LAW'S TWO APARTMENTS. HE OWNED BOTH, AND HE GAVE TO ME PART OWNERSHIP AND A VERY BEAUTIFUL GOLD WATCH FOR A WEDDING GIFT.

BUT THIS WHAT I JUST TOLD YOU—ABOUT LUCIA AND SO—I DON'T WANT YOU SHOULD WRITE THIS IN YOUR BOOK.

WHAT? WHY NOT?

IT HAS NOTHING TO DO WITH HITLER, WITH THE HOLOCAUST!

BUT POP—IT'S GREAT MATERIAL. IT MAKES EVERYTHING MORE REAL—MORE HUMAN.

I WANT TO TELL YOUR STORY, THE WAY IT REALLY HAPPENED.

BUT THIS ISN'T SO PROPER, SO RESPECTFUL.

... I CAN TELL YOU OTHER STORIES, BUT SUCH PRIVATE THINGS, I DON'T WANT YOU SHOULD MENTION.

OKAY, OKAY— I PROMISE.

## CHAPTER TWO

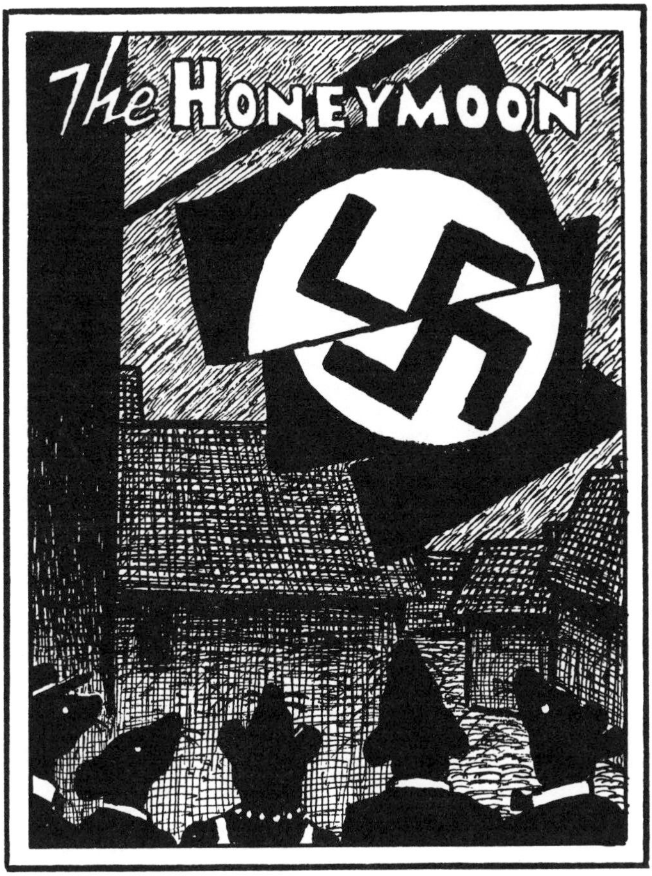
The Honeymoon

For the next few months I went back to visit my father quite regularly, to hear his story.

ABOUT MOM....

...11...12...13...

-UH... WHAT ARE YOU DOING, POP?

I'M MAKING INTO DAILY PORTIONS MY PILLS. ...14...15...

...16...17...18...

SO MANY?

IT'S 6 PILLS FOR THE HEART, 1 FOR DIABETES... AND MAYBE 25 OR 30 VITAMINS.

FOR MY CONDITION I MUST FIGHT TO *SAVE* MYSELF. DOCTORS, THEY ONLY GIVE ME "JUNK FOOD"...

..THAT'S HOW I CALL PRESCRIPTION DRUGS NOW. I STUDY THIS IN MY *PREVENTION* MAGAZINES... MAYBE YOU WANT TO READ?

NO THANKS.

ABOUT MOM - DID SHE HAVE ANY BOYFRIENDS BEFORE SHE MET YOU?

NOT **ROMANTIC**... BUT *ONE* TALL BOY FROM WARSAW

HE WAS... A **COMMUNIST!**

26

EVEN AFTER THE MARRIAGE, WHEN THIS FELLOW CAME TO SOSNOWIEC, ANJA ALWAYS RAN TO SEE HIM.

I DIDN'T KNOW, OF COURSE, THAT HE WAS COMMUNIST. I **ALWAYS** KEPT FAR AWAY FROM COMMUNIST PEOPLE.

A LITTLE AFTER WE WERE MARRIED I CAME HOME FROM A SELLING TRIP...

HEY VLADEK-THEY JUST ARRESTED THE SEAMSTRESS THAT LIVES DOWN YOUR HALL!...

SHE HAD SOME SECRET COMMU-NIST DOCUMENTS!

AND WHEN I WENT UPSTAIRS...

THE POLICE JUST ARRES-HUH? WHAT'S THE MATTER?

THE POLICE WERE **HERE!**

LOOKING FOR ANJA!

SHE JUST TOLD US...

THAT BOY FROM WARSAW BRINGS COMMUNIST MESSAGES.

SHE TRANSLATES THEM INTO GERMAN AND PASSES THEM ON!

ANJA WAS INVOLVED IN *CONSPIRATIONS!*

A LITTLE BEFORE THE POLICE CAME, SHE GOT FROM FRIENDS A TELEPHONE CALL...

THEY SUSPECT YOU! HIDE THE PAPERS QUICKLY! BUT THEY'RE IMPORTANT—TRY NOT TO DESTROY THEM.

WHAT TO DO? SHE RAN TO THE SEAMSTRESS WHAT WAS ONE OF OUR TENANTS

MISS STEFANSKA—*PLEASE!* HIDE THIS PACKAGE FOR ME—DON'T TELL *ANYONE* ABOUT IT!

?

AND ANJA WAS A GOOD CUSTOMER, SO SHE AGREED.

THE POLICE WENT OVER *OUR* HOUSE TOP TO BOTTOM. IT WAS NOTHING TO FIND SO THEY SEARCHED THE NEIGHBORS.

OKAY—HOW DID YOU GET THIS PACKAGE?

I NEVER SAW IT BEFORE—ONE OF MY CUSTOMERS MUST HAVE LEFT IT!

ANJA WAS SAFE, BUT THE SEAMSTRESS THEY ARRESTED.

WHEN I FOUND OUT THIS STORY, I WAS READY TO BREAK THE MARRIAGE.

I TOLD HER "ANJA, IF YOU WANT ME YOU HAVE TO GO MY WAY...

IF YOU WANT YOUR COMMUNIST FRIENDS, THEN I CAN'T STAY IN THIS HOUSE!"

AND SHE WAS A GOOD GIRL, AND OF COURSE SHE STOPPED ALL SUCH THINGS.

WHAT HAPPENED TO THE SEAMSTRESS?

MISS STEFANSKA SAT IN PRISON FOR A LONGER TIME – MAYBE 3 MONTHS.

IT WASN'T ENOUGH EVIDENCE AND FINALLY THE POLICE LEFT HER GO.

FATHER-IN-LAW PAID THE COST FROM THE LAWYERS AND GAVE TO HER SOME MONEY–IT COST MAYBE 15,000 ZLOTYS.

THAT'S A LOT, HUH?

JA, BUT NOT ONLY THIS. AT THE SAME TIME HE DID FOR US EVEN *MORE*...

YOU KNOW, VLADEK, WHEN YOU AND ANJA GIVE ME A GRANDCHILD, I WANT HIM TO BE WELL-OFF.

WELL, I ALMOST HAVE ENOUGH FROM MY SALES TRIPS TO START UP A TEXTILE SHOP...

A SHOP? PFUI! YOU OUGHT TO HAVE A TEXTILE *FACTORY!*

THAT WOULD COST A *FORTUNE!!*

*PLEASE* – I CAN GIVE YOU THE MONEY AND PLENTY OF CREDIT.

I STARTED A FACTORY IN *BIELSKO*, AND VISITED TO ANJA EVERY WEEK-END.

BY OCTOBER 1937, THE FACTORY WAS GOING, AND IT WAS BORN MY FIRST SON, RICHIEU.

HE'S A BIG BABY- OVER 3 KILOS.

MY GOD.. ANJA ONLY WEIGHS 39!

OF COURSE, YOU NEVER KNEW HIM. HE DIDN'T COME OUT FROM THE WAR.

YES, I KNOW...

BUT WAIT- IF YOU WERE MARRIED IN FEBRUARY, AND RICHIEU WAS BORN IN OCTOBER, WAS HE PREMATURE?

YES, A LITTLE...

BUT *YOU*- AFTER THE WAR, WHEN YOU WERE BORN- IT WAS *VERY* PREMATURE. THE DOCTORS THOUGHT YOU WOULDN'T LIVE.

I FOUND A *SPECIALIST* WHAT SAVED YOU... HE HAD TO BREAK YOUR *ARM* TO TAKE YOU OUT FROM ANJA'S BELLY!

AND WHEN YOU WERE A TINY BABY YOUR ARM ALWAYS JUMPED UP, LIKE *SO!*

WE JOKED AND CALLED YOU "HEIL HITLER!"

ALWAYS WE PUSHED YOUR ARM DOWN, AND YOU WOULD OOPS!

LOOK *NOW* WHAT YOU MADE ME DO!

*ME?* OKAY, I'LL RE-COUNT THEM LATER.

*NO!* YOU DON'T *KNOW* COUNTING PILLS. I'LL DO IT AFTER... I'M AN *EXPERT* FOR THIS.

SO... ANJA STAYED WITH THE FAMILY AND I WENT TO LIVE IN BIELSKO FOR MY FACTORY BUSINESS AND TO FIND FOR US AN APARTMENT...

BUT SOON IT CAME FROM SOSNOWIEC A TELEPHONE...

VLADEK! COME HOME RIGHT AWAY - ANJA IS *SICK!*

SHE WAS CRYING AS SOON I CAME IN...

WHAT'S WRONG, DARLING?

SOB

IT DOESN'T MATTER... *NOTHING* MATTERS.

BUT WHY ARE YOU CRYING?

I DON'T *KNOW!* I HAVE A GOOD FAMILY... A FINE SON.. I SHOULD BE *HAPPY...*

BUT I DON'T CARE. *I JUST DON'T WANT TO LIVE.*

HERE, BABY. DRINK THIS AND REST.

I DON'T UNDERSTAND. WHAT'S THE MATTER?

GIVING BIRTH WAS TOO MUCH OF A STRAIN. SHE'S ALWAYS HYSTERICAL OR DEPRESSED... A *BREAKDOWN!*

PLEASE

THE DOCTOR TOLD US ABOUT A SANITARIUM.

... BUT SOMEBODY MUST GO WITH HER... SOMEONE SHE TRUSTS.

EVERYTHING'S ARRANGED - THE CHILD CAN STAY HERE WITH A GOVERNESS.

... AND I'LL WATCH YOUR FACTORY.

SOB

31

RIGHT AWAY, WE WENT. THE SANITARIUM WAS INSIDE CZECHOSLOVAKIA, ONE OF THE MOST EXPENSIVE AND BEAUTIFUL IN THE WORLD.

I REMEMBER WHEN WE WERE ALMOST ARRIVED, WE PASSED A SMALL TOWN.

OI!

EVERYBODY-EVERY JEW FROM THE TRAIN- GOT VERY EXCITED AND FRIGHTENED.

LOOK!

IT WAS THE BEGINNING OF 1938-BEFORE THE WAR- HANGING HIGH IN THE CENTER OF TOWN, IT WAS A NAZI FLAG..

HERE WAS THE FIRST TIME I SAW, WITH MY OWN EYES, THE SWASTIKA.

I TELL YOU, THERE'S A POGROM GOING ON IN GERMANY TODAY!

ONE FELLOW TOLD US OF HIS COUSIN WHAT WAS LIVING IN GERMANY...

...HE HAD TO SELL HIS BUSINESS TO A GERMAN AND RUN OUT FROM THE COUNTRY WITHOUT EVEN THE MONEY.

I AM A FILTHY JEW

IT WAS VERY HARD THERE FOR THE JEWS-TERRIBLE!

ANOTHER FELLOW TOLD US OF A RELATIVE IN BRANDENBERG - THE POLICE CAME TO HIS HOUSE AND NO ONE HEARD AGAIN FROM HIM.

This town is Jew Free

IT WAS MANY, MANY SUCH STORIES - SYNAGOGUES BURNED, JEWS BEATEN WITH NO REASON, WHOLE TOWNS PUSHING OUT ALL JEWS - EACH STORY WORSE THAN THE OTHER.

LET'S HOPE THOSE NAZI GANGSTERS GET THROWN OUT OF POWER!

JUST PRAY THAT THEY DON'T START A WAR!!

33

THE SANITARIUM WAS FAR AWAY FROM EVERYTHING— SO PEACEFUL, SO QUIET.

LOOK AT HOW BEAUTIFUL THESE GARDENS ARE, ANJA.

UH HUH

PEOPLE CAME FROM ALL OVER THE WORLD WITH DIFFERENT SICKNESS- ES. IT WAS EVEN SHOPS HERE.... A THEATER... REALLY BEAUTIFUL...

OUR ROOM IS LIKE A LUXURY HOTEL—LOOK AT THIS VIEW.

UH HUH

EACH MORNING NURSES WOULD VISIT TO ANJA.

AND EACH FEW DAYS I TALKED TO THE BIG SPECIALIST AT THE CLINIC.

WELL, WHAT DID THE DOCTOR SAY??

HE TOLD ME YOU'RE DOING FINE...FINE..

JUST RELAX.

I UNDERSTOOD MUCH OF SUCH SICKNESSES, SO I HELPED ALWAYS TO CALM HER DOWN.

LOOK—WE GOT A LET- TER FROM HOME TODAY.

WITH A PHOTO OF RICHIEU—LET ME SEE.

HE'S A HANDSOME BOY... JUST LIKE HIS FATHER, YES?

YES.

IN THE EVENINGS WE WENT EITHER TO THE THEATER OR TO DANCE IN THE CAFE.

DID I TELL YOU THE TRAGEDY ABOUT THE PILLOW MY FAMILY LOST AT THE START OF THE 1914 WAR! I WAS SEVEN.... WE LIVED TOO CLOSE TO THE BORDER ... IT WASN'T SAFE...

I TOLD HER MANY JOKES AND STORIES TO KEEP HER BUSY...

...SO WE TOOK WHAT WE COULD ON A WAGON PULLED BY FOUR HORSES AND WENT TO MY GRANDFATHER'S HOME IN RADOMSKO.

SOMEONE RODE PAST US AND TOLD US THAT WE'D DROPPED A PILLOW A FEW MILES BACK. A GUY TRAVELING TO AMSTOW PICKED IT UP.

IMAGINE - MY FATHER NEVER RODE A HORSE BEFORE ... BUT HE UNHITCHED ONE FROM THE WAGON AND RODE TOWARD AMSTOW..

WE WAITED AND WAITED.. MOTHER STARTED CRYING: "SURELY HE FELL AND GOT KILLED!" SHE HAD BEGGED HIM TO "LET THE PILLOW GO AND TAKE ALL OUR TROUBLES WITH IT!"

THE HORSE WAS BONY AND DIDN'T HAVE A SADDLE... FINALLY, LATE THAT NIGHT, FATHER RODE BACK WITH THE PILLOW ...UNDER HIS BLOODY *TUCHUS*...

SO, FATHER GOT HIS PILLOW BACK ...BUT HE COULDN'T SIT DOWN FOR THE REST OF THE WAR!

I LOVE YOU, VLADEK.

AND SHE WAS SO LAUGHING AND SO HAPPY, SO HAPPY, THAT SHE APPROACHED EACH TIME AND KISSED ME, SO HAPPY SHE WAS.

WE STAYED MAYBE 3 MONTHS, AND WHEN WE CAME BACK, ANJA WAS COMPLETELY DIFFERENT FROM WHEN SHE LEFT.

YOO HOO, POPPA!

ANJA! YOU LOOK LIKE A MILLION!

LISTEN, VLADEK... I DIDN'T WANT YOU TO WORRY WHILE YOU WERE AT THE SANITARIUM, BUT —

—BRACE YOURSELF—THE BIELSKO FACTORY HAS BEEN ROBBED!

WHAT!

IT HAPPENED LAST MONTH. THEY TOOK EVERYTHING!

AI! AI! AI!

I DIDN'T EVEN HAVE TIME TO INSURE IT BEFORE WE LEFT.

WELL, AT LEAST I CAN HELP YOU BUILD IT UP AGAIN.

WERE YOU LOOTED AS PART OF SOME KIND OF ANTI-SEMITIC ACTIVITY?

I DON'T THINK THIS WAS IT. JUST A ROBBERY....

...LIKE WHEN THEY ROBBED US IN REGO PARK HERE, LAST YEAR.

WELL.... IN BIELSKO, FATHER-IN-LAW HELPED US AGAIN TO ESTABLISH OURSELVES ...

IN A COUPLE MONTHS WE WERE WELL-OFF— *QUITE* WELL-OFF.... A WORKING FACTORY, A 2 BEDROOM APARTMENT, A POLISH GOVERNESS, AND EVEN A MAID.

LOOK, RICHIEU, POPPA'S HOME!

YOU LOOK UPSET, VLADEK.

THERE WAS ANOTHER RIOT DOWNTOWN TODAY.

...EVERYONE YELLING, "JEWS OUT! JEWS OUT!"...EVEN TWO PEOPLE KILLED. THE POLICE JUST WATCHED!

IT'S THOSE NAZIS STIRRING EVERYBODY UP!

WHEN IT COMES TO JEWS, THE POLES DON'T *NEED* MUCH STIRRING UP!

MRS. SPIEGELMAN— HOW CAN YOU SAY SUCH A THING. I THINK OF YOU AS PART OF MY OWN FAMILY!

I'M SORRY, JANINA. I DIDN'T MEAN *YOU!* I'M JUST WORRIED!

MAYBE WE SHOULD MOVE AWAY, LIKE SOME OTHERS HAVE.

IF THINGS GET *REALLY* BAD WE'LL RUN BACK TO SOSNOWIEC.

WHY WOULD SOSNOWIEC BE ANY SAFER THAN BIELSKO?

WE THOUGHT THEN, THAT HITLER WANTED ONLY THE PARTS FROM POLAND, LIKE BIELSKO, WHAT USED TO BE PARTS FROM GERMANY BEFORE THE FIRST WORLD WAR.

WE WERE VERY HAPPY, STILL, FOR OVER A YEAR—UNTIL AUGUST 24, 1939.

A LETTER—FROM THE GOVERNMENT!

A DRAFT NOTICE! I WAS IN THE POLISH RESERVES ARMY, AND SO I HAD TO GO RIGHT AWAY!

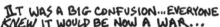

IT WAS A BIG CONFUSION...EVERYONE KNEW IT WOULD BE NOW A WAR...

QUICK! PACK EVERYTHING! YOUR FATHER WILL TAKE YOU TO SOSNOWIEC.

VLADEK, I'M AFRAID!

GRAB YOUR KNICK-KNACKS, AND THE DOLL COLLECTION!

THEY'RE NOT IMPORTANT!

YOU'LL SEE. YOU MAY ENJOY THEM.

I WAS RIGHT. WHEN THINGS WENT WORSE LATER, SHE WAS ABLE TO SELL SUCH THINGS.

SO ANJA AND RICHIEU AND THE GOVERNESS WENT IN ONE WAY—TO SOSNOWIEC...

...AND I WENT THEN IN A DIFFERENT DIRECTION...TO THE FRONTIER AGAINST GERMANY.

..AND ON SEPTEMBER 1, 1939, THE WAR CAME. I WAS ON THE FRONT, ONE OF THE FIRST TO ACH!

SO. TWICE I SPILLED MY DRUGSTORE!

IT'S MY EYES.

EVER SINCE I GOT IN MY LEFT EYE THE HEMORRHAGING AND THE GLAUCOMA, IT HAD TO BE TAKEN OUT FROM ME. AND NOW I DON'T SEE SO WELL.

AND NOW I HAVE A CATARACT INSIDE MY ONE GOOD EYE. YOU SEE HOW I HAVE TO SUFFER?

I TOLD YOU ABOUT THE BIG-SHOT SPECIALIST WHAT WAS GOING TO OPERATE ME?

UH-HUH.

HE LAST YEAR PUT ME INTO THE HOSPITAL FOR AN IMMEDIATE OPERATION...

AND THEN HE JUST LEFT ME.. HE WENT SOMEWHERE AWAY TO GIVE LECTURES, ON THE TELEVISION!

MY EYE STARTED SO BLEEDING, I HAD TO RUN OUT TO FIND A DOCTOR IN A DIFFERENT HOSPITAL.

THERE ANOTHER SPECIALIST OPERATED RIGHT AWAY! OTHERWISE I COULD HAVE DIED.

SO NOW ITS A GLASS EYE.

HE DID A GOOD JOB, NO? ONE TIME, EVEN, A YOUNG DOCTOR CAME TO MY BED THERE IN THE HOSPITAL...

HE LOOKED WITH A LIGHT A LONG TIME IN MY EYES AND TOLD: "MR. SPIEGELMAN, YOUR LEFT EYE IS PERFECT!...

"...BUT IN YOUR RIGHT EYE IS CATARACTS."

HE DIDN'T KNOW, OF COURSE, THAT THE LEFT EYE IS GLASS...

AND I DIDN'T TELL ANYTHING TO HIM. I DIDN'T WANT TO MAKE HIM AN EMBARRASSMENT.

UH-HUH — YOU TOLD ME ABOUT THAT.

WELL, IT'S ENOUGH FOR TODAY, YES? I'M TIRED AND I MUST COUNT STILL MY PILLS.

OKAY, GOOD IDEA... MY HAND IS SORE FROM WRITING ALL THIS DOWN.

# CHAPTER THREE

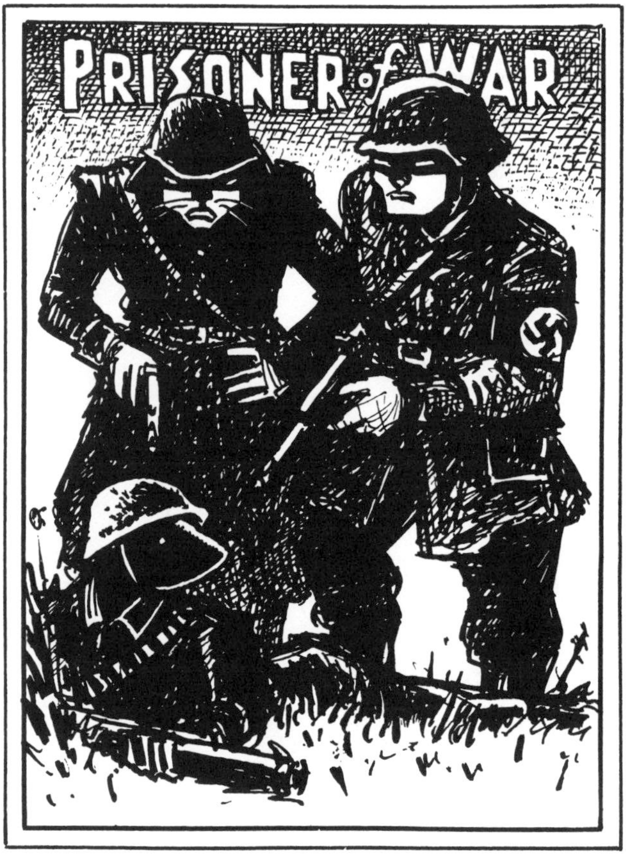
PRISONER of WAR

I visited my father more often in order to get more information about his past..

HAVE SOME MORE GREEN BEANS, ARTIE.

YES, LOOK - YOU DON'T EAT ANYTHING!

NO THANKS, I'VE HAD ENOUGH.

SO FINISH AT LEAST WHAT'S ON YOUR PLATE!

OKAY... OKAY.

Y'KNOW, MALA, WHEN I WAS LITTLE, IF I DIDN'T EAT EVERYTHING MOM SERVED, POP AND I WOULD ARGUE TIL I RAN TO MY ROOM CRYING ...

YOU SHOULD KNOW IT'S IMPOSSIBLE TO ARGUE WITH YOUR FATHER.

...MOM WOULD OFFER TO COOK SOMETHING I LIKED BETTER, BUT POP JUST WANTED TO LEAVE THE LEFTOVER FOOD AROUND UNTIL I ATE IT.

SOMETIMES HE'D EVEN SAVE IT TO SERVE AGAIN AND AGAIN UNTIL I'D EAT IT OR STARVE.

YES! SO IT HAS TO BE. ALWAYS YOU MUST EAT ALL WHAT IS ON YOUR PLATE.

ACCH, VLADEK.

43

FORTUNATELY FOR ME, MOM WOULD EVENTUALLY FEED ME SOMETHING I LIKED, AND THROW AWAY THE OLD FOOD WHILE YOU WEREN'T LOOKING.

YES. ANJA WAS TOO EASY WITH YOU ALWAYS.

HMMH. THANKS FOR THE DINNER, MALA. IT WAS DELICIOUS.

PFEH — THE CHICKEN WAS, I THOUGHT, TOO DRY. COME, WE'LL TALK BETTER IN THE LIVING ROOM.

OKAY — I'LL GET MY NOTEBOOK.

...I TELL YOU, WITH MALA I DON'T KNOW WHAT TO DO. SHE—

PLEASE, POP! I'D RATHER NOT HEAR ALL THAT *AGAIN*. TELL ME ABOUT 1939, WHEN YOU WERE DRAFTED.

1939? YES...WE WERE GIVEN ARMY TRAININGS FOR A FEW DAYS AND THEN, BY THE START OF SEPTEMBER WE WERE ON THE FRONTIER.

...WE WERE ALL DIGGED INTO TRENCHES NEAR A RIVER. ON THE OTHER SIDE IT WAS GERMANS.

44

IT WAS EVERYTHING QUIET UNTIL NEAR MORNING...

WAIT A MINUTE. THEY ONLY TRAINED YOU FOR A FEW **DAYS** BEFORE SENDING YOU INTO COMBAT!

WELL, THE **FIRST** TIME I WENT INTO THE ARMY FOR 18 MONTHS WHEN I WAS 21. THEN EVERY 4 YEARS I WENT TO LUBLIN FOR A MONTH TO TRAIN.

YOU KNOW, MY **FATHER** TRIED TO KEEP ALL HIS CHILDREN **OUT** FROM THE ARMY..

..BECAUSE WHEN **HE** WAS YOUNG, HE HAD THEN TO GO INTO THE **RUSSIAN** ARMY. ...AND THERE THEY TOOK YOU FOR 25 YEARS. ...TO **SIBERIA**!

MY FATHER PULLED OUT 14 OF HIS **TEETH** TO ESCAPE. IF YOU MISSED 12 TEETH THEY LEFT YOU GO.

SO WHEN MY BROTHER **MARCUS** GOT 21 YEARS, FATHER PUT HIM ON A STARVATION DIET. ALWAYS MARCUS WAS SICKLY-SO THIN.

AND WHEN HE WENT FOR THE ARMY EXAMINATION...THEY DIDN'T TAKE HIM.

A YEAR LATER WHEN IT CAME **MY** TURN, FATHER WANTED TO MAKE TO ME THE SAME THING.

IT WAS SOMETHING **TERRIBLE!**...

45

THREE MONTHS BEFORE THE EXAMINATION HE STARTED WITH ME...

WAKE UP, VLADEK! YOU'RE SLEEPING TOO MUCH!

ONLY THREE HOURS A NIGHT?

STOP, VLADEK. YOU MUSTN'T EAT SO MUCH!

BUT I'M HUNGRY!

OKAY— HAVE ONE MORE HERRING.

FOR THREE MONTHS I ATE ONLY SALTED HERRING AND NO WATER TO LOSE WEIGHT.

AND A FEW DAYS BEFORE THE EXAM, *NO* SLEEP AND *NO* FOOD...

GOOD BOY—JUST A LITTLE MORE COFFEE!

ONLY A GALLON COFFEE A DAY FOR MY HEART.

AND WHEN FINALLY I WENT FOR MY MEDICAL EXAMINATION...

HERE'S A HEALTHY ONE.

UM!...

NO...THERE SEEMS TO BE *SOMETHING* WRONG WITH HIM.

BUILD YOURSELF UP FOR A YEAR, YOUNG MAN, AND WE'LL REVIEW YOUR CASE AGAIN.

...THE NEXT YEAR FATHER WANTED I WOULD _AGAIN_ DO THE SAME THING. BUT I BEGGED HIM AND WENT IN 1922 TO THE ARMY...

·BUT LET'S GET BACK TO 1939!

YES. YOU SEE HOW YOU MIX ME UP? ...IN 1939 WE WERE ON THE FRONTIER, DIGGED INTO TRENCHES BY A RIVER.

IT WAS QUIET UNTIL NEAR MORNING. THEN I HEARD SHOOTING ON BOTH SIDES.

AN OFFICER SNEAKED OVER TO ME.

DIG IN DEEPER. YOU'LL GET KILLED.

YOUR GUN IS COLD! WHY AREN'T YOU SHOOTING?

I DIDN'T SEE AT _WHAT_ TO SHOOT...

KPOK! KPOK! KPOK!

...BUT I DIGGED DEEPER AND STARTED TO SHOOT!

THEN BULLETS CAME IN MY DIRECTION.

I DUG *DEEPER* MY TRENCH BUT I STOPPED TO SHOOT.

BUT WHEN I LOOKED IN MY GUN, I SAW... A TREE!!!!

AND THE TREE WAS ACTUALLY MOVING!

WELL, IF IT MOVED, I HAD TO SHOOT!

IT HELD UP A HAND TO SHOW IT WAS HURT. TO SURRENDER.

BUT I KEPT SHOOTING AND SHOOTING. UNTIL FINALLY THE TREE STOPPED MOVING. WHO KNOWS; OTHERWISE HE COULD HAVE SHOT ME!

AFTER TWO HOURS OF FIGHTING, THE NAZIS OVERCAME OUR SIDE OF THE RIVER.

GET UP!

GIVE ME YOUR GUN!

IT'S *HOT!* YOU WERE SHOOTING AT US!

MY COMMANDER *MADE* ME SHOOT. I ONLY FIRED IN THE AIR!

I ANSWERED IN GERMAN AND HIS PARTNER STOPPED HIM FROM BEATING ME.

THEY MARCHED ME TO WHERE IT WAS MORE LIKE ME. WAR PRISONERS.

AND ALL FROM US WHAT WEREN'T INJURED THEY MARCHED OVER TO THEIR SIDE OF THE RIVER TO LOOK FOR DEAD SOLDIERS.

49

ATTENTION! ALL PRISONERS WILL CARRY OUR DEAD AND WOUNDED TO THE WAITING RED CROSS TRUCKS.

YOU! WHERE DO YOU THINK YOU'RE GOING?

I-I THOUGHT I SAW A BODY OVER BY THE RIVER!

I KNEW WHERE THE ONE I SHOT SHOULD BE LAYING.

YES. HERE!

ER VERBLUTETE! HIS BLOOD RAN OUT! CARRY HIM OVER TO THE TRUCK WITH THE OTHERS.

HIS NAME WAS JAN...

... AND I KNEW THAT I KILLED HIM.

AND I SAID TO MYSELF: "WELL, AT LEAST I DID SOMETHING."

THEY TOOK US TO A PLACE NEAR NUREMBERG WHERE IT WAS **MANY** WAR PRISONERS. THE JEWS THEY MADE TO STAND SEPARATE.

IT'S ALL **YOUR** FAULT, THIS WAR!

WE SHOULD **HANG** YOU RIGHT HERE ON THIS SPOT!

OF COURSE, NOBODY OF US SAID A WORD.

PUT DOWN ALL YOUR VALUABLES!

HE CAME UP TO ME... I HAD MAYBE 300 ZLOTYS.

WHY SO MUCH MONEY, JEW?

MANY OTHERS HAD ONLY 5 OR 6 ZLOTYS.

DO YOU EXPECT TO DO SOME **BUSINESS** HERE?

SHOW ME YOUR HANDS!

YOU NEVER WORKED A DAY IN YOUR LIFE!

LIKE YOU, ARTIE, MY HANDS WERE ALWAYS VERY DELICATE.

WELL, JEW, DON'T WORRY. WE'LL FIND WORK FOR YOU!

AND THEY DID.

ANOTHER GERMAN TOOK 4 OR 5 FROM US TO A STABLE.

SEE THIS MESS? IT BETTER BE SPOTLESSLY CLEAN IN ONE HOUR. UNDERSTAND!

IT WAS IMPOSSIBLE TO DO IT IN ONE HOUR!

WE REALLY WORKED VERY HARD. BUT, AN HOUR LATER...

SO!

NOT FINISHED YET?

THIS WILL COST YOU YOUR SOUP, YOU LAZY BASTARDS!

AND SOMEHOW WE DID MAKE THE JOB IN ONLY AN HOUR AND A HALF. BUT LOOK WHAT YOU DO, ARTIE!

HUH?

YOU'RE DROPPING ON THE CARPET CIGARETTE ASHES. YOU WANT IT SHOULD BE LIKE A STABLE HERE?

OOPS. SORRY.

CLEAN IT, YES? OTHERWISE I HAVE TO DO IT. MALA COULD LET IT SIT LIKE THIS FOR A WEEK AND NEVER TOUCH IT.

AND SHE KNOWS HOW WITH MY SICKNESSES IT'S HARD NOW FOR ME TO DO SUCH THINGS.

OKAY, OKAY. IT'S CLEAN.

SO WE LIVED AND WORKED A FEW WEEKS IN THE STABLE UNTIL THEY TOOK US TO AN EVEN *BIGGER* PRISONER OF WAR CAMP.

BRRR. THE POLISH PRISONERS GET *HEATED* CABINS.

YES, AND WE'RE JUST LEFT TO FREEZE IN THESE TENTS.

IT WAS TERRIBLE COLD THAT AUTUMN. ALL OVER EUROPE IT WAS SO FREEZING THAT BIRDS FELL FROM TREES.

TO KEEP WARM WE HAD ONLY OUR SUMMER UNIFORMS AND A THIN BLANKET.

AT LEAST IF THEY GAVE US ENOUGH TO EAT.

THE OTHER PRISONERS GET *TWO* MEALS A DAY. WE JEWS GET ONLY A CRUST OF BREAD AND A LITTLE SOUP.

GOOD MORNING, VLADEK.

WHERE ARE YOU GOING?

TO BATHE IN THE RIVER.

YOU'VE GONE CRAZY.

≥BRR≤ I'LL BE *CLEAN*! AND I'LL FEEL WARM ALL DAY BY COMPARISON.

MANY OTHERS GOT FROSTBITE WOUNDS. IN THE WOUNDS WAS PUS, AND IN THE PUS WAS LICE.

53

EVERY DAY I BATHED AND DID GYMNASTICS TO KEEP STRONG. ...AND EVERY DAY WE PRAYED.

OFTEN WE PLAYED CHESS TO KEEP OUR MINDS BUSY AND MAKE THE TIME GO.

AND ONE TIME A WEEK WE COULD WRITE LETTERS THROUGH THE INTERNATIONAL RED CROSS.

מה־טובו אהליך
יעקב, משכנתיך
ישראל.

I WAS VERY RELIGIOUS, AND IT WASN'T *ELSE* TO DO.

I HAD A SET MADE FROM STONES AND BREAD CRUMBS.

Dear Anja,
I am fine.
I miss you.

ONLY IN GERMAN. AND VERY CAREFUL.

AND THROUGH THIS IT CAME A PACKAGE...

CHOCOLATE BARS! CIGARETTES! JAM!

IT WAS SO TREASURING FOR ME THIS PACKAGE.

I HAD A SIGN MY FAMILY WAS SAFE, AND— BECAUSE I NEVER SMOKED—I HAD CIGARETTES TO TRADE FOR FOOD.

AND SO THINGS WENT FOR MAYBE SIX WEEKS, THEN...

LOOK! THERE'S AN ANNOUNCE- MENT OUTSIDE!

**WORKERS NEEDED**
War Prisoners may volun- teer for labor assignments to replace German work- ers called to the front. Housing and abundant food will be supplied.

IT'S A TRICK!

NEVER VOLUNTEER!

IF WE *HAVE* TO DIE, LET'S DIE *HERE*!

NO!

I DIDN'T AGREE!

I'M NOT GOING TO DIE, AND I WON'T DIE HERE! I WANT TO BE TREATED LIKE A HUMAN BEING!

WHEN MY COMRADES SAW I WAS GOING, THEY TOO REGISTERED.

WE WERE RIGHT AWAY SENT TO A BIG GERMAN COMPANY.

WE WERE TAKEN TO NICE WOODEN HOUSES. WE GOT SOUP AND WE GOT BREAD...

LOOK! A STOVE!

AND REAL BEDS!

WITH SHEETS AND PILLOWS!

AND FOR A WHOLE DAY WE ONLY RESTED AND GOT BACK OUR STRENGTH.

AH- IT SEEMS LIKE YEARS SINCE I'VE FELT WARM OR BEEN IN A BED!

YES- FUNNY, ISN'T IT? IT'S ONLY A LITTLE OVER 2 MONTHS SINCE WE WERE DRAFTED.

I'M WORRIED THOUGH, VLADEK- WHO KNOWS WHAT KIND OF WORK THEY'LL GIVE US.

IT DOESN'T MATTER..

.. ANYTHING IS BETTER THAN ROTTING IN THOSE TENTS.

I SUPPOSE.

THE NEXT DAY WE WERE GIVEN SHOVELS AND PICKS ....

..."THINGS WHAT WE NEVER HELD IN OUR HANDS BEFORE.

AND THE WORK WAS REALLY VERY HARD— WE HAD TO MOVE MOUNTAINS.

MOUNTAIN

VALLEY

THE HILLS WERE MAYBE 3 OR 4 YARDS HIGH. WE HAD TO MAKE IT LEVEL.

SOME COMPLAINED—THOSE WHAT WERE TOO OLD OR WEAK FOR SUCH WORK:

I-I CANT TAKE ANYMORE.

WORTHLESS JEW!

IF YOU'RE UNHAPPY—GO BACK TO THE P.O.W. CAMP.

IT'S OKAY—WE'LL HELP YOU WHEN NO ONE IS LOOKING.

WE TRIED TO HELP, BUT—WHAT YOU THINK?—SOME WENT BACK TO THE TENTS TO FREEZE AND TO STARVE.

BUT WHAT HAP- PENED TO THEM, I DON'T KNOW.

STILL, EIGHTY PER CENT STAYED. THERE WAS ENOUGH TO EAT, AND A WARM BED. IT WAS BETTER TO STAY...

...ALWAYS I WENT TO SLEEP EXHAUSTED. AND ONE NIGHT I HAD A DREAM...

"DON'T WORRY...

A VOICE WAS TALKING TO ME. IT WAS, I THINK, MY DEAD GRANDFATHER...

"...DON'T WORRY, MY CHILD..."

IT WAS SO REAL, THIS VOICE...

"YOU WILL COME OUT OF THIS PLACE — FREE! ...ON THE DAY OF PARSHAS TRUMA."

I WOKE UP RIGHT AWAY. AND WHEN I WENT TO SLEEP, AGAIN IT WAS: "PARSHAS TRUMA! PARSHAS TRUMA!"

SO WHAT'S PARSHAS TRUMA?

EACH WEEK, ON SAT-URDAY, WE READ A SEC-TION FROM THE TORAH.

THIS IS SO CALLED — A PARSHA... AND ONE WEEK EACH YEAR IT IS PARSHAS TRUMA.

BEFORE WORK A FEW FROM US PRAYED. IT WAS A RABBI THERE WITH US.

ONE MOMENT, RABBI. WHEN WILL WE READ PARSHAS TRUMA?

PARSHAS TRUMA?..

...IN THE MIDDLE OF FEB-RUARY — ALMOST THREE MONTHS FROM NOW. WHY?

THREE MONTHS — AND EVERY DAY WAS FOR US A YEAR!

I TOLD HIM MY DREAM...

LET'S HOPE IT'S TRUE. I'M AFRAID WE'LL NEVER GET OUT OF HERE.

57

SO WE WORKED, DAY AFTER DAY. WE SURVIVED. WEEK AFTER WEEK. THE SAME.

UNTIL, ONE TIME...

LOOK— SOLDIERS!

IT CAME VERY MANY GESTAPO AND WEHRMACHT.

ATTENTION! LINE UP ON THE ROAD IN TWO ROWS! IMMEDIATELY!

WE WERE NOT AT EASE. WE DIDN'T KNOW WHAT THEY COULD DO WITH US.

I STOOD ALWAYS IN THE SECOND LINE.

(PSST—VLADEK.)

I DIDN'T WANT THEY SHOULD SEE ME MUCH.

SOMEONE SNEAKED NEXT TO ME...

RABBI! DO YOU KNOW WHAT DAY IT IS?

SATURDAY, OF COURSE.

BUT DO YOU KNOW WHAT A SATURDAY?...

IT'S PARSHAS TRUMA!

58

THEY MARCHED US TO THE MAIN COURTYARD AND LINED US BY ALPHABET AT TABLES...

NAME AND RANK?

SPIEGELMAN, VLADEK. CORPORAL.

DESTINATION UPON RELEASE?

SOSNOWIEC...

THIS THE GERMANS DID VERY GOOD...

...TO MY WIFE AND CHILD.

...ALWAYS THEY DID EVERY THING VERY SYSTEMATIC.

VERY WELL— SIGN THIS RELEASE FORM.

...AND IT WAS ALL DONE IN ONE DAY.

YOU MEAN YOUR 'PARSHAS TRUMA' DREAM ACTUALLY CAME TRUE?

YES—THIS IS FOR ME A VERY IMPORTANT DATE...

I CHECKED LATER ON A CALENDAR. IT WAS THIS PARSHA ON THE WEEK I GOT MARRIED TO ANJA.

...AND THIS WAS THE PARSHA IN 1948, AFTER THE WAR, ON THE WEEK YOU WERE BORN!...

AND SO IT CAME OUT TO BE THIS PARSHA YOU SANG ON THE SATURDAY OF YOUR BAR MITZVAH!

THE NEXT MORNING EACH FROM US GOT A RED CROSS PACKAGE, AND THEY LOADED US ON A TRAIN TO POLAND.

DURING THE JOURNEY I SAT WITH THE RABBI.

SO, MY SON. NOW I SEE YOU ARE A "ROH-EH HANOLED," ONE WHO SEES WHAT THE FUTURE WILL BRING.

HEY! THIS TRAIN SEEMS TO BE PASSING SOSNOWIEC!

WHEN THEY DIDN'T STOP THE TRAIN I BECAME VERY WORRIED.

YOU SEE, THE NAZIS DIVIDED POLAND INTO PIECES: PROTECTORATE AND REICH, WITH A GUARDED BORDER BETWEEN.

BALTIC SEA
LITHUANIA
E. PRUSSIA
( annexed to Russia )
POLAND
GERMANY
SOVIET UNION
WARSAW
LUBLIN
SOSNOWIEC
KRAKOW
SLOVAKIA
HUNGARY
RUMANIA

REICH: Annexed to Germany

PROTECTORATE: German controlled Government.

THE TRAIN WENT COMPLETELY PAST MY PART OF POLAND—THE REICH—AND STOPPED ONLY IN THE PROTECTORATE.

THOSE WITH PAPERS FOR KRAKOW—OUT!

AND, WHEN IT STOPPED IN WARSAW, THE RABBI GOT OUT.

I'LL WRITE TO YOU.

BUT I NEVER HEARD AGAIN FROM HIM. IT CAME SUCH A MISERY IN WARSAW, ALMOST NONE SURVIVED.

AND THE TRAIN WAS A LONG WAY PAST SOSNOWIEC. THEY TOOK ME UP, UP, VERY FAR—MAYBE 300 MILES—UNTIL WE CAME TO LUBLIN. THERE THEY UNLOADED ALL OF US FROM THE REICH.

60

IN LUBLIN, THEY TOOK US TO BIG TENTS...

AND THERE WE SAT.

EVENTUALLY CAME SOME PEOPLE TO SEE US FROM THE JEWISH AUTHORITIES....

WHY ARE WE BEING KEPT HERE?

IT'S A VERY BAD SITUATION... JUST BEFORE YOU ARRIVED, THERE WAS ANOTHER GROUP OF RELEASED WAR PRISONERS...

...TWO DAYS AGO THE NAZIS MARCHED THEM TO A FOREST,...

...AND THEY SHOT ALL OF THEM—THEY KILLED 600 PEOPLE!

WE WERE THE NEXT PARTY!

I THOUGHT YOU WERE RELEASED AS A PRISONER OF WAR!

EXACTLY SO..

INTERNATIONAL LAWS PROTECTED US A LITTLE AS POLISH WAR PRISONERS. BUT A JEW OF THE REICH, ANYONE COULD KILL IN THE STREETS!

THEN WE HEARD SOMETHING TO GIVE US A LITTLE HOPE....

WE'VE BRIBED THE GERMANS TO RELEASE PRISONERS INTO THE HOMES OF LOCAL JEWS WHO WILL CLAIM YOU AS RELATIVES.

MY NAME'S SPIEGELMAN. THERE'S A FRIEND OF MY FAMILY NAMED ORBACH IN LUBLIN. I MET HIM WHEN I WAS HERE FOR ARMY TRAINING.

FINE! WE'LL TRY TO REGISTER YOU AS HIS COUSIN.

THAT NIGHT I WENT OUT FROM THE TENT...

I HAD TO URINATE.

I RAN QUICK INSIDE ....

AND A GUARD BEGAN SHOOTING TO ME.

AND THOUGHT ALL NIGHT DIFFERENT THINGS WHAT COULD HAPPEN TO US.

THEN, AS SOON AS IT WAS LIGHT...

SPIEGELMAN!..
SPIEGELMAN!..

VLADEK!

ORBACH! AM I GLAD TO SEE YOU!

AND IN TEN MINUTES, I WAS FREE!

ORBACH WAS A FRIEND FROM MY UNCLE—HE HAD TWO BEAUTIFUL DAUGHTERS NEAR TO MY AGE.

I'M SORRY WE CAN'T OFFER YOU A BETTER MEAL, VLADEK—BUT THE JEWS OF LUBLIN GET VERY FEW FOOD COUPONS.

ONE MOMENT, GIRLS—I HAVE A GIFT FOR EACH OF YOU...

OH MY GOD! CHOCOLATE!

THESE I SAVED FROM A RED CROSS PACKAGE. ALWAYS I SAVED... JUST IN CASE!

EVENTUALLY, WHEN I CAME AGAIN TO SOSNOWIEC, WE SENT THEM FOOD PACKAGES...

...WE WERE FOR A WHILE A LITTLE BETTER OFF... AND THEY WROTE BACK VERY HAPPY HOW IT HELPED SURVIVE THEM...

...THEN THEY WROTE THAT THE GERMANS WERE KEEPING THE PACKAGES, AND THEN THEY STOPPED TO WRITE. FINISHED.

WITH ORBACHS' I STAYED A FEW DAYS RECUPERATING. BUT I WAS RESTLESS. HOW COULD I MANAGE TO SNEAK ACROSS THE BORDER TO MY FAMILY?

...BUT ANYWAY I GOT ON THE TRAIN IN THE DIRECTION I WANTED.

I APPROACHED TO THE TRAIN MAN, A POLE...

MAY I TALK TO YOU FOR A MOMENT?

SURE, SOLDIER.

I STILL HAD ON MY ARMY UNIFORM, AND I DIDN'T LET *KNOW* I WAS A JEW.

YOU'RE A POLE LIKE ME, SO I CAN TRUST YOU... THE STINKING NAZIS HAD ME IN A WAR PRISON... I JUST ESCAPED.

THE POLES WERE VERY BITTER ON THE GERMANS, SO IT WAS GOOD TO SPEAK BAD OF THEM.

I'M TRYING TO GET TO SOSNOWIEC — BACK TO MY FAMILY.

DON'T WORRY... WHEN WE GET TO THE BORDER, HIDE IN HERE.

AND SO THE TRAIN MAN HELPED ME COME BACK TO MY SIDE OF POLAND.

I WALKED FIRST OVER TO MY PARENTS' HOUSE...

...WHAT I THOUGHT I MIGHT NEVER SEE AGAIN.

OY GEVALT! IT'S **VLADEK!**

MY SON! THANK GOD YOU'RE SAFE!

AND IN SPITE OF EVERYTHING, YOU LOOK *HEALTHY!*

I'M STRONG, MOTHER. BUT *YOU* LOOK SICK!

IT'S BECAUSE I WAS WORRIED ABOUT YOU.

BUT IT WASN'T ONLY THIS. SHE WAS SICK OF CANCER.

... AND A MONTH OR TWO LATER, SHE DIED.

SHE NEVER KNEW HOW TERRIBLE EVERYTHING WOULD SOON BE!

—AND, FATHER! YOUR BEARD! WHAT HAPPENED? YOU *SHAVED IT OFF?!??*

IT'S GROWING BACK, NOW...

HE WAS VERY RELIGIOUS—SO LIKE A RABBI—AND, OF COURSE, HE ALWAYS HAD A BIG BEARD.

IN SEPTEMBER THE GERMAN SOLDIERS GRABBED MANY JEWS IN THE STREET...

THEY MADE US SING PRAYERS WHILE THEY LAUGHED AND BEAT US.

...AND BEFORE LETTING US GO, THEY CUT OFF OUR BEARDS.

AND NOW THE DEMONS HAVE TAKEN AWAY MY SELTZER FACTORY. THEY—

ENOUGH!

I MUST BRING VLADEK HOME TO ANJA BEFORE CURFEW.

AT 7:00 IT WAS A RULE. ALL JEWS HAD TO BE IN THEIR HOME. AND ALL LIGHTS OUT.

FROM MY PARENTS' TO SOSNOWIEC WAS ONLY A SHORT RIDE.

GO IN AND SAY YOU JUST GOT A LETTER FROM ME SAYING I'D BE HOME IN A WEEK.

I STOOD AT THE DOOR, LISTENING...

DON'T JOKE! IF VLADEK WAS COMING HOME, HE'D HAVE WRITTEN TO US TOO!

SURPRISE!

OH MY GOD.

VLADEK!

I GRABBED MY SON. HE WAS 2½ YEARS.

RICHIEU!

BWAAH

HE STARTED SCREAMING.

WHY DO YOU CRY, MY BOY? I'M YOUR FATHER!

WAH

:SNF: TH' BUTTONS, YOUR METAL BUTTONS, DADDY—THEY'RE COLD!

AND I DON'T NEED TO TELL YOU HOW BIG THE JOY WAS IN OUR HOUSE.

EVEN THOUGH EVERYTHING WAS VERY TOUGH—AND IT WAS REALLY VERY TOUGH—WE WERE HAPPY ONLY TO BE TOGETHER.

..NOT SO LIKE IT IS NOW WITH ME AND MALA.

I TELL YOU, IF ANJA COULD BE ALIVE NOW, IT WOULD BE EVERYTHING DIFFERENT WITH ME!

MALA MAKES ME CRAZY. ONLY SHE TALKS ABOUT MONEY. ALWAYS ABOUT MY WILL—

PLEASE, POP! ...

YOU ALWAYS TELL ME THE SAME THINGS. THERE'S NOTHING I CAN DO.

BUT I HAVEN'T WITH WHOM ELSE TO TALK!

AND IT'S FOR YOU I WATCH OUT MY MONEY!

JEEZ—LET'S TALK ABOUT IT NEXT TIME. I'LL CALL YOU!

BESIDES, IT'S GETTING LATE. I OUGHTA GET HOME BEFORE CURFEW!

HMF.

HEY—WHERE'S MY COAT? I KNOW I PUT IT IN HERE!

67

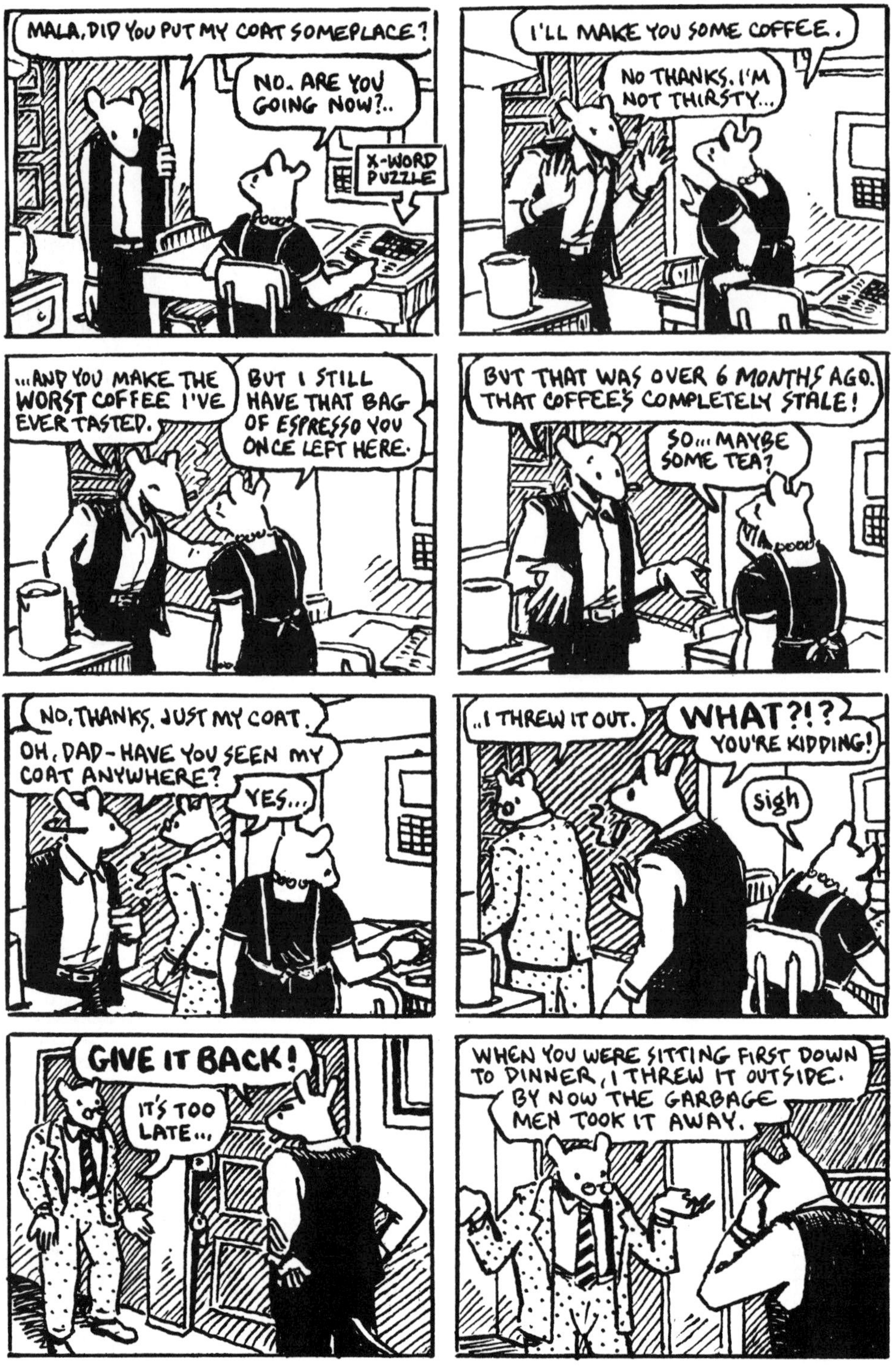
MALA, DID YOU PUT MY COAT SOMEPLACE?
NO. ARE YOU GOING NOW?..
X-WORD PUZZLE
I'LL MAKE YOU SOME COFFEE.
NO THANKS. I'M NOT THIRSTY...
...AND YOU MAKE THE WORST COFFEE I'VE EVER TASTED.
BUT I STILL HAVE THAT BAG OF ESPRESSO YOU ONCE LEFT HERE.
BUT THAT WAS OVER 6 MONTHS AGO. THAT COFFEE'S COMPLETELY STALE!
SO... MAYBE SOME TEA?
NO, THANKS. JUST MY COAT.
OH, DAD - HAVE YOU SEEN MY COAT ANYWHERE?
YES...
..I THREW IT OUT.
WHAT?!? YOU'RE KIDDING!
sigh
GIVE IT BACK!
IT'S TOO LATE...
WHEN YOU WERE SITTING FIRST DOWN TO DINNER, I THREW IT OUTSIDE. BY NOW THE GARBAGE MEN TOOK IT AWAY.

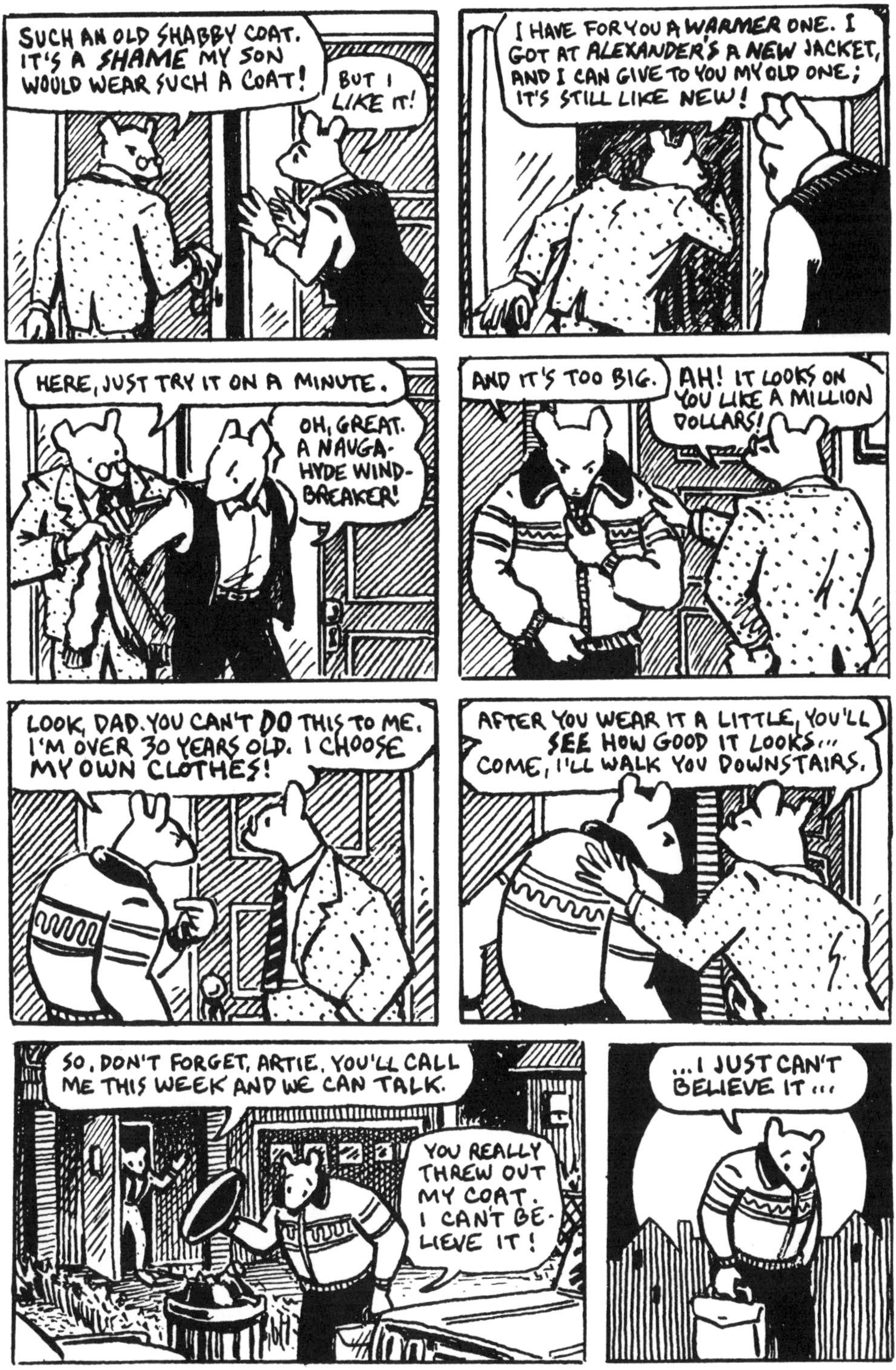
SUCH AN OLD SHABBY COAT. IT'S A SHAME MY SON WOULD WEAR SUCH A COAT!
BUT I LIKE IT!
I HAVE FOR YOU A WARMER ONE. I GOT AT ALEXANDER'S A NEW JACKET, AND I CAN GIVE TO YOU MY OLD ONE; IT'S STILL LIKE NEW!
HERE, JUST TRY IT ON A MINUTE.
OH, GREAT. A NAUGA-HYDE WIND-BREAKER!
AND IT'S TOO BIG.
AH! IT LOOKS ON YOU LIKE A MILLION DOLLARS!
LOOK, DAD. YOU CAN'T DO THIS TO ME. I'M OVER 30 YEARS OLD. I CHOOSE MY OWN CLOTHES!
AFTER YOU WEAR IT A LITTLE, YOU'LL SEE HOW GOOD IT LOOKS... COME, I'LL WALK YOU DOWNSTAIRS.
SO, DON'T FORGET, ARTIE, YOU'LL CALL ME THIS WEEK AND WE CAN TALK.
YOU REALLY THREW OUT MY COAT. I CAN'T BE-LIEVE IT!
...I JUST CAN'T BELIEVE IT...

# CHAPTER FOUR

THE NOOSE TIGHTENS

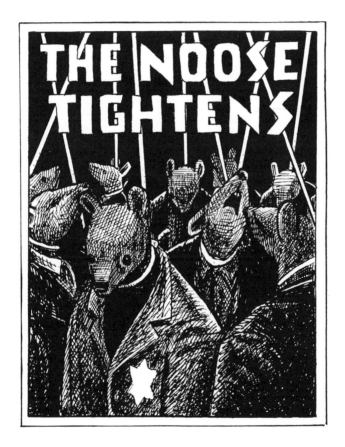

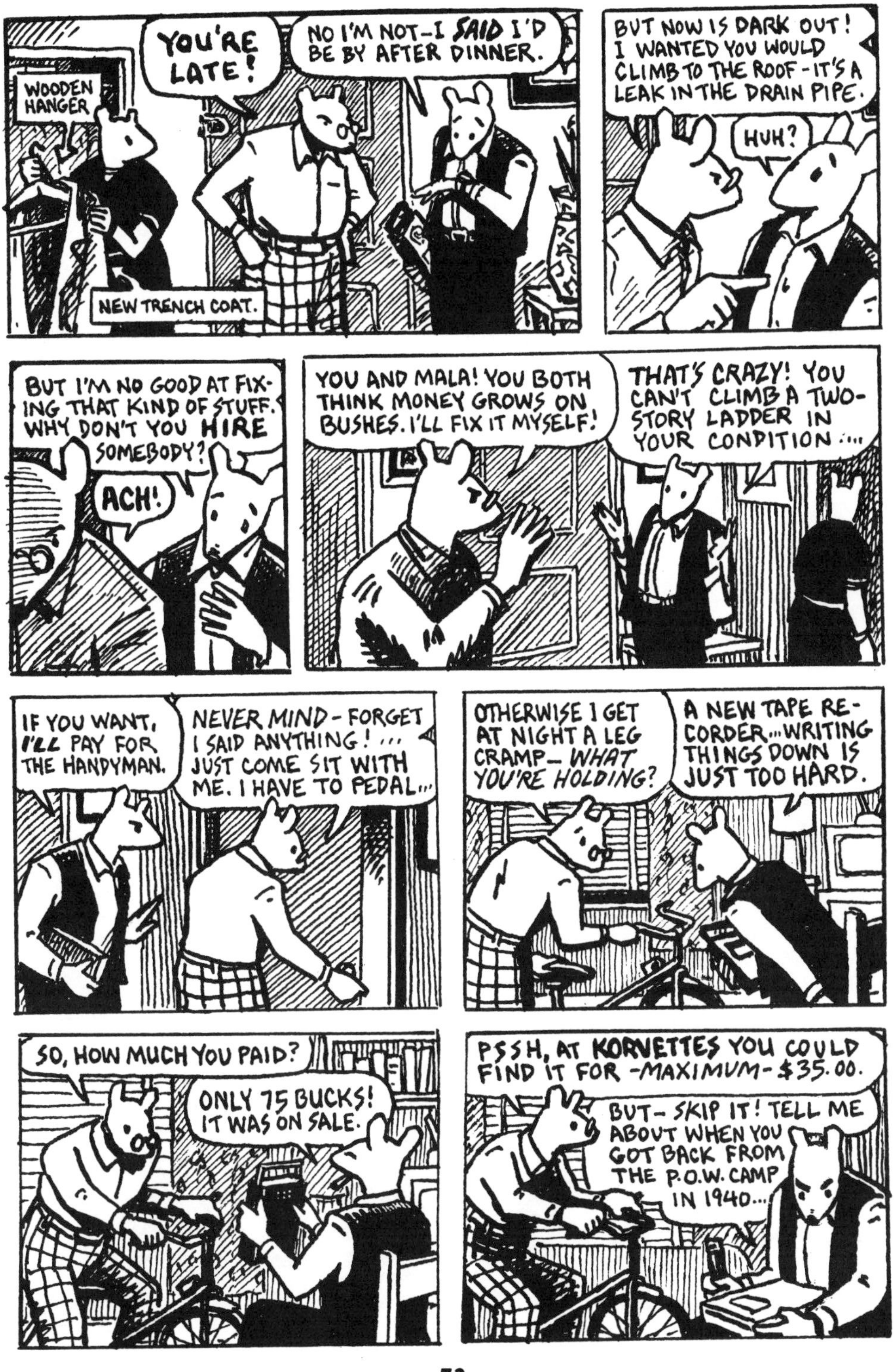

WOODEN HANGER
YOU'RE LATE!
NO I'M NOT—I SAID I'D BE BY AFTER DINNER.
NEW TRENCH COAT.
BUT NOW IS DARK OUT! I WANTED YOU WOULD CLIMB TO THE ROOF - IT'S A LEAK IN THE DRAIN PIPE.
HUH?
BUT I'M NO GOOD AT FIXING THAT KIND OF STUFF. WHY DON'T YOU HIRE SOMEBODY?
ACH!
YOU AND MALA! YOU BOTH THINK MONEY GROWS ON BUSHES. I'LL FIX IT MYSELF!
THAT'S CRAZY! YOU CAN'T CLIMB A TWO-STORY LADDER IN YOUR CONDITION....
IF YOU WANT, I'LL PAY FOR THE HANDYMAN.
NEVER MIND - FORGET I SAID ANYTHING!... JUST COME SIT WITH ME. I HAVE TO PEDAL...
OTHERWISE I GET AT NIGHT A LEG CRAMP— WHAT YOU'RE HOLDING?
A NEW TAPE RECORDER... WRITING THINGS DOWN IS JUST TOO HARD.
SO, HOW MUCH YOU PAID?
ONLY 75 BUCKS! IT WAS ON SALE.
PSSH, AT KORVETTES YOU COULD FIND IT FOR -MAXIMUM- $35.00.
BUT- SKIP IT! TELL ME ABOUT WHEN YOU GOT BACK FROM THE P.O.W. CAMP IN 1940...

WHEN FIRST I CAME HOME IT LOOKED EXACTLY SO AS BEFORE I WENT AWAY...

IT WAS STILL VERY LUXURIOUS. THE GERMANS COULDN'T DESTROY EVERYTHING AT ONE TIME.

IT WAS TWELVE OF US LIVING IN FATHER-IN-LAW'S HOUSEHOLD...

IT WAS ANJA AND ME, AND OUR BOY, RICHIEU...

ANJA'S OLDER SISTER, TOSHA, HER HUSBAND, WOLFE, AND THEIR LITTLE GIRL, BIBI...

AND IT WAS ANJA'S GRAND-PARENTS. THEY HAD MAYBE 90 YEARS, BUT VERY ALERT...

AND, OF COURSE, IT WAS MY FATHER-IN-LAW AND MY MOTHER-IN-LAW...

AND ALSO THE 2 KIDS FROM YOUR UNCLE HERMAN AND AUNT HELEN: LOLEK AND LONIA

HERMAN AND HELA WERE LUCKY. THEY WERE VISIT-ING THE N.Y. WORLD'S FAIR WHEN THE WAR CAME.

THIS SAVED THEM.

74

AH, GRANDMOTHER - YOUR STEW IS EVEN TASTIER THAN I REMEMBERED.

NO - IT'S NOT LIKE BEFORE THE WAR, VLADEK - I CAN'T GET THE FOODS I NEED.

EACH OF US GETS COUPONS FOR 8 OUNCES OF BREAD A DAY, AND A TINY BIT OF MARGARINE, SUGAR AND JAM PER WEEK. THAT'S ALL!

SO HOW DO WE MANAGE?

I'VE DONATED A LOT TO THE GEMEINDE - THE JEWISH COMMUNITY ORGANIZATION - AND WOLFE WORKS THERE... SO WE GET A LITTLE EXTRA.

AND THERE'S THE BLACK MARKET.

WITH MONEY YOU CAN ALWAYS GET ANYTHING!

IT'S DANGEROUS, THOUGH. THE NAZIS TAKE YOU OFF TO A WORK CAMP FOR BREAKING ANY MINOR LAW.

WORSE - EVEN IF YOU DON'T BREAK ANY LAWS!

... AND THOSE THAT ARE TAKEN AWAY - THEY'RE NEVER SEEN AGAIN!

WELL, WE SHOULD BE HAPPY WE'RE ALL TOGETHER WITH ENOUGH TO EAT.

BUT WE MUST REALLY TIGHTEN OUR BELTS UNTIL THE WAR ENDS.

COME-LET'S PLAY RUMMY WHILE THE LADIES CLEAR THE TABLE.

HAS THE FAMILY BEEN TAKING GOOD CARE OF MY BIELSKO TEXTILE FACTORY?

DON'T YOU KNOW? ..ALL JEWISH BUSINESSES HAVE BEEN TAKEN OVER BY "ARYAN MANAGERS"...

I WENT TO OUR FACTORY IN LODZ, AND THEY SAID, "BETTER GO HOME TODAY, OLD MAN...TOMORROW WE'LL CARRY YOU OUT."

WHAT?

BUT ISN'T ANY MONEY COMING IN?

NOT A SINGLE ZLOTY. AND THE FAMILY WANTS TO LIVE THE WAY IT DID BEFORE THE WAR!

OKAY, VLADEK-CUT THE CARDS.

BUT, WOLFE-WHAT KIND OF WORK ARE YOU DOING?

JUST A LITTLE OFFICE WORK FOR THE GEMEINDE ... BUT A FEW MONTHS AGO FATHER-IN-LAW TOOK ALL HIS VALUABLES HOME FROM THE BANK SAFE.

HOW LONG CAN SAVINGS LAST?

DON'T WORRY SO MUCH, VLADEK. YOU'LL SEE ... THE WAR WILL BE OVER LIKE LIGHTNING!

JA! LIKE LIGHTNING!

ACH!

WOLFE LOOKED ONLY TO PLAY CARDS.

I WENT THE NEXT DAY TO MODRZEJOWSKA STREET. HERE PEOPLE STILL MADE MONEY, FROM *SECRET* BUSINESSES... NOT SO LEGAL...

(PSST— FOOD COUPONS FOR REICHSMARKS?)

VLADEK SPIEGELMAN!

MR. ILZECKI! WHAT ARE YOU DOING IN SOSNOWIEC?

ILZECKI USED TO BE A CUSTOMER OF MINE... THE BEST TAILOR IN KATOWICE.

THE NAZIS MOVED ME TO AN APARTMENT HERE. I MAKE UNIFORMS FOR THEIR OFFICERS... AND SUITS ON THE SIDE WHEN I CAN GET THE CLOTH.

ARE YOU STILL IN BUSINESS?

I DON'T KNOW. I *JUST* GOT BACK FROM WAR PRISON.

WELL, IF YOU GET ANY CLOTH, COME SEE ME. THIS NOTE WILL GET YOU PAST THE DOORMAN.

THE NOTE TOLD THAT I WORKED WITH HIM. SUCH A PAPER COULD BE USEFUL TO HAVE.

I WENT THEN TO SHOPS WHAT STILL OWED ME MONEY FROM BEFORE THE WAR...

BUT I *CAN'T* PAY YOU! A GERMAN RUNS MY PLACE NOW. I'M LUCKY JUST TO HAVE A JOB!

THEN ADVANCE ME A FEW YARDS OF MATERIAL WITHOUT COUPONS.

OKAY, OKAY. HIDE THIS UNDER YOUR CLOTHES.

MR. ILZECKI, PLEASE.

SO I MADE A NICE FEW ZLOTYS THE VERY FIRST WEEK I CAME HOME.

I REMEMBER, FATHER-IN-LAW WAS *SO* HAPPY WITH ME.

YOU SEE, AT LEAST THERE'S *ONE* SMART GUY IN THE FAMILY.

OF COURSE I ONLY SAID I GOT *HALF* WHAT I REALLY MADE. OTHERWISE THEY WOULDN'T *SAVE* ANYTHING.

A LITTLE LATER I WAS AGAIN ON MODRZEJOWSKA, LOOKING TO BUY SOME TEXTILES WITHOUT COUPONS...

...THE S.S. CLOSED OFF THE WHOLE STREET TO INSPECT THE WORKING PAPERS FROM EVERYONE.

I DIDN'T *KNOW* BEFORE ABOUT THIS.

I MANAGED TO DISAPPEAR INTO A BUILDING.

BUT THEY TOOK MAYBE 50% OF THE PEOPLE AWAY.

I TALKED ABOUT IT TO FATHER-IN-LAW...

THEY ALMOST GOT ME! I'LL NEED MORE THAN JUST ILZECKI'S NOTE!

IT'S TRUE.

COME... WE'LL VISIT A FRIEND OF MINE WHO OWNS A TIN SHOP. I THINK HIS OVERSEER CAN BE BRIBED.

AND SO IT WENT...

OKAY, VLADEK... SINCE WE MAKE THINGS FOR GERMANY WE CAN GET YOU A PRIORITY WORK CARD.

REMEMBER, IF THERE'S A ROUND-UP, RUN IN HERE AND PRETEND YOU'RE WORKING.

I LEARNED HERE TO DO THINGS WHAT WERE USEFUL TO ME WHEN I CAME TO AUSCHWITZ.

AND SO WE LIVED FOR MORE THAN A YEAR. BUT ALWAYS THINGS CAME A LITTLE WORSE, A LITTLE WORSE...

FATHER-IN-LAW HAD A NICE NEW BEDROOM SET...

THE GERMANS LOOKED TO *GRAB* SUCH FURNITURE, BECAUSE IN STORES IT WASN'T ANYMORE TO GET.

WOLFE AND I SHLEPPED EVERYTHING VALUABLE DOWNSTAIRS FOR A POLISH NEIGHBOR TO HIDE.

OOF. ARE WE LEAVING THE OTHER BED UPSTAIRS?

JA. MOTHER-IN-LAW IS TOO SICK. SHE *NEEDS* A GOOD BED.

ANJA'S MOTHER HAD GALLSTONES. THE DAY THE GERMANS CAME SHE LAY IN THE BED.

PLEASE DON'T TAKE HER BED—LOOK AT HOW SICK SHE IS.

THE DOCTOR IS HERE EVERY DAY.

FATHER-IN-LAW HAD AN OLD FRIEND WHO CAME ALWAYS OVER TO PLAY CARDS.

...AND THEY LEFT WITHOUT TAKING *ANYTHING!*

YOU KNOW, I MET A GERMAN OFFICIAL WHO WOULD PAY WELL FOR A BEDROOM SET...

HIDDEN, WE HAD NO USE FROM THE FURNITURE. SO WE SHLEPPED IT AGAIN UPSTAIRS TO SELL.

YOU HAVE EXCELLENT TASTE IN FURNITURE, HERR ZYLBERBERG. THANK YOU.

MY MEN WILL BE RIGHT BACK TO GET YOUR *WIFE'S* BED TOO!...

YOU *CHEATED* US LAST TIME, JEW!

WAIT! I HAVEN'T BEEN PAID, YET.

PLEASE, IF YOU WANT TO STAY ALIVE GO BACK INSIDE.

HE WAS SO UNHAPPY AFTER. SO UNHAPPY!

79

ONE TIME I WAS GOING TO SEE ILZECKI. THIS WAS LATE IN 1941, I THINK. HIS HOUSE WAS VERY NEAR TO A TRAIN STATION...

... AND IT WAS GOING ON THERE SOMETHING **TERRIBLE**.

I HAD TO PASS NEAR—AND THEY WERE GRABBING JEWS, IF THEY HAD PAPERS OR NO!

WHAT HAD I TO DO?

WILL I WALK SLOWLY, THEY WILL TAKE ME...

WILL I *RUN* THEY CAN SHOOT ME!

THEN FROM FAR, I SAW ILZECKI WALKING, SO I WENT HASTY OVER TO HIM.

ALLO!

MR. SPIEGELMAN! WHAT ARE YOU DOING HERE? DON'T YOU SEE WHAT'S GOING ON?

QUICK—COME UPSTAIRS WITH ME UNTIL THE TRAINS LEAVE!

ILZECKI LIVED IN A VERY FANCY HOUSE. HE WAS THE ONLY JEW THERE.

SO I SAT WITH HIM AND HIS WIFE A GOOD FEW HOURS. WE HEARD SHOOTING AND SCREAMS.

HE SURVIVED ME MY LIFE THAT TIME.

ILZECKI HAD A SON THE SAME AGE LIKE RICHIEU. IF YOU ONLY COULD SEE HOW THOSE CHILDREN PLAYED TOGETHER.

LISTEN, VLADEK..

WE CAN'T KNOW WHAT'S GOING TO HAPPEN TO *US* - BUT WE *MUST* KEEP OUR CHILDREN SAFE.

I HAVE A GOOD FRIEND, A POLE, WHO'S WILLING TO HIDE MY SON UNTIL THE SITUATION GETS BETTER.

...I THINK HE'D TAKE YOUR BOY TOO.

YES, YOU MAY BE RIGHT! LET ME SPEAK WITH MY FAMILY.

BUT, I'M TELLING YOU, IT WAS SOMETHING **TERRIBLE** GOING ON IN OUR HOUSE WHEN I EVEN *MENTIONED* IT.

**WHAT?** HAVE YOU GONE **CRAZY**?

HOW CAN YOU EVEN **THINK** OF GIVING RICHIEU UP TO COMPLETE STRANGERS?!

I'LL *NEVER* GIVE UP MY BABY. NEVER!

ILZECKI AND HIS WIFE DIDN'T COME OUT FROM THE WAR.

...BUT HIS SON REMAINED ALIVE; OURS DID NOT.

...AND **ANYWAY** WE HAD TO GIVE RICHIEU TO HIDE A YEAR LATER.

WHEN WE WERE IN THE GHETTO, IN 1943, TOSHA TOOK ALL THE CHILDREN TO—

WAIT! PLEASE, DAD. IF YOU DON'T KEEP YOUR STORY CHRONOLOGICAL, I'LL NEVER GET IT STRAIGHT... TELL ME MORE ABOUT 1941 AND 1942.

SO?... OKAY. I'LL MAKE IT SO HOW YOU WANT IT. 1941?... AT THE END OF 1941 THE GERMANS CAME WITH SOMETHING NEW. WOLFE RAN FROM THE GEMEINDER...

LOOK! THEY'RE PUTTING THESE UP ALL OVER TOWN.

**ORDER**
All Jews of Sosnowiec must be relocated into the Stara Sosnowiec quarter by January 1, 1942. Non-Jews will be moved into vacated premises.

Monek Merin

ALL 12 OF OUR HOUSEHOLD WERE GIVEN NOW TO LIVE IN 2½ SMALL ROOMS...

REWARD
FOR EVERY UNREGISTERED JEW YOU FIND: 1 KILO of SUGAR

MOST PEOPLE GOT EVEN *LESS* SPACE. BUT FATHER-IN-LAW AND WOLFE HAD A LITTLE *INFLUENCE*...

BUT THIS WASN'T YET A REAL GHETTO. STILL YOU COULD GO INTO OTHER PARTS OF TOWN SO LONG YOU WERE HOME AT NIGHT-TIME

HOLD THE LADDER, ANJA.

I'M PUTTING UP A CURTAIN TO GIVE US SOME PRIVACY.

TOSHA *INSISTED* ON GETTING THE PART OF THE ROOM WITH THE WINDOW.

IT DOESN'T MATTER, VLADEK. I'M JUST GLAD THE WHOLE FAMILY CAN STAY TOGETHER.

IT WAS NO MORE THE LUXURY LIFE WE HAD BEFORE.

FOR A COUPLE MONTHS I DID HERE STILL MY BLACK MARKET BUSINESS. THEN CAME MORE BAD NEWS, VERY BAD...

WHAT'S WRONG, FATHER?

THEY JUST ARRESTED MY FRIEND, NAHUM COHN, AND HIS SON.

THEY'VE TAKEN *FOUR* JEWS AWAY FOR DEALING GOODS WITHOUT COUPONS.

I DID MUCH BUSINESS WITH COHN!

THE GERMANS INTEND TO MAKE AN *EXAMPLE* OF THEM!

THE NEXT DAY I WALKED OVER TO MODRZEJOWSKA STREET AND I SAW THEM...

THEY HANGED THERE ONE FULL WEEK.

COHN HAD A DRY GOODS STORE. HE WAS KNOWN OVER ALL SOSNOWIEC. OFTEN HE GAVE ME CLOTH WITH NO COUPONS.

I TRADED ALSO WITH PFEFER, A FINE YOUNG MAN—A ZIONIST. HE WAS JUST MARRIED. HIS WIFE RAN SCREAMING IN THE STREET.

I WAS FRIGHTENED TO GO OUTSIDE FOR A FEW DAYS... I DIDN'T WANT TO PASS WHERE THEY WERE HANGING.

AND MAYBE ONE OF THEM COULD HAVE TALKED OF ME TO THE GERMANS TO TRY TO SAVE HIMSELF.

ACH. WHEN I THINK NOW OF THEM, IT STILL MAKES ME CRY... LOOK—EVEN FROM MY DEAD EYE TEARS ARE COMING OUT!

WHAT WAS ANJA DOING AT AROUND THIS TIME?

HOUSEWORKS... AND KNITTING... READING... AND SHE WAS WRITING ALWAYS HER DIARY.

I USED TO SEE POLISH NOTEBOOKS AROUND THE HOUSE AS A KID. WERE THOSE HER DIARIES?

YES, AND ALSO NO.

HER DIARIES DIDN'T SURVIVE FROM THE WAR. WHAT YOU SAW SHE WROTE AFTER: HER WHOLE STORY FROM THE START.

OHMIGOD! WHERE ARE THEY? I NEED THOSE FOR THIS BOOK!

COFF! PLEASE, ARTIE, STOP WITH THE SMOKING. IT MAKES ME SHORT WITH BREATH.

I THINK IT'S ALL YOUR PEDALING!

DON'T BE SO SMART! ... WHAT I WAS TELLING YOU? YES... AFTER THE HANGING I LOOKED FOR ANOTHER BUSINESS ...

... I STARTED TO TRADE GOLD AND JEWELRY.

IT WAS EASIER TO HIDE THAN CLOTHINGS. I KEPT THINGS HIDDEN IN THE CHILD'S STROLLER, AND I MADE A FEW ZLOTYS.

FOR A WHILE I HAD ALSO A FOOD BUSINESS THAT I DIDN'T YET TELL YOU...

I MET SZKLARCZYK. HE HAD A BIG GROCERY ON MODRZEJOWSKA...

YOU'RE ZYLBERBERG'S SON-IN-LAW, RIGHT? COME INSIDE AND WAIT FOR THE RAIN TO STOP.

SO, TOGETHER WE SAT AND SPOKE, AND HE HELPED, FROM TIME TO TIME, A CUSTOMER...

SORRY - YOU DON'T HAVE ENOUGH COUPONS TO BUY ½ KILO OF SUGAR.

STILL... SHE WENT OUT WITH ½ KILO. I SMELLED I COULD ARRANGE SOMETHING.

THEN A LITTLE MORE WE SPOKE AND HE MADE TO ME A PROPOSITION...

MAYBE YOU COULD SELL MY "EXTRA" ITEMS TO SMALL SHOPS IN THE AREA ...UNDER THE COUNTER.

IT WAS DANGEROUS TO CARRY THESE THINGS - BUT MAYBE I COULD BE LUCKY.

WHEN SOMEBODY IS HUNGRY HE LOOKS FOR BUSINESS...

ONE TIME I HAD 10 OR 15 KILOS SUGAR TO DELIVER...

HALT, JEW! WHAT ARE YOU CARRYING?

WHAT WAS I SUPPOSED TO SAY? FOR THIS I COULD REALLY HANG!

SUGAR.

...I'M TAKING IT OVER TO MY GROCERY STORE.

OH. YOU HAVE A SHOP?

I MADE SO THEY WOULD THINK IT WAS LEGAL.

I WENT TO THE BACK DOOR WHERE I HAD TO DELIVER...

OPEN UP, POLDEK!

..I'VE GOT OUR SUGAR.

?!

AND THEY LEFT ME GO WITHOUT EVEN CHECKING MY PAPERS!

BUT WHEN WE CAME TO STARA SOSNOWIEC, ALL MY BUSINESSES BECAME HARDER... IT WAS NOT SO EASY TO MOVE AROUND.

THE TIN SHOP FINISHED—THE OWNER WAS THE ONLY JEW THEY LET WORK THERE. I GOT THEN A JOB IN A GERMAN CARPENTRY SHOP.

FATHER-IN-LAW AND LOLEK WORKED ALREADY THERE, FOR REALLY NO MONEY. I DIDN'T NEED THIS BEFORE, BUT NOW I HAD TO HAVE THE WORK PAPER.

WOLFE COULD HAVE ARRANGED ME A JOB AT THE GEMEINDE... BUT I DIDN'T WANT TO PUT MY HANDS THERE WHERE JEWS WERE BEING TAKEN.

AND THEN IT CAME **AGAIN** SOMETHING NEW FROM THE GERMANS. WE GOT A NOTICE...

"ALL JEWS OVER 70 YEARS OLD WILL BE TRANSFERED TO THERESIENSTADT IN CZECHOSLOVAKIA ON MAY 10, 1942..."

"...A COMMUNITY BETTER PREPARED TO TAKE CARE OF THE ELDERLY THAN OURS IN SOSNOWIEC...;"

IT DOESN'T LOOK TOO BAD!

LIKE A CONVALESCENT HOME.

NOTICE:

ANJA'S GRANDPARENTS HAD ABOUT 90 YEARS.

WE'VE BEEN TOGETHER —A FAMILY—FOR 70 YEARS. WE DON'T WANT TO BREAK APART NOW!

DON'T WORRY. WE WON'T LET THEM TAKE YOU.

WE DIDN'T YET **KNOW** OF AUSCHWITZ—OF THE OVENS—BUT WE WERE **ANYWAY** AFRAID.

...SO, IN THE YARD, WE MADE A HIDING PLACE, A BUNKER...

CUT-AWAY VIEW:

STORAGE SHEDS

FALSE WALL

GRAND-PARENTS

WE SNEAKED FOOD TO THEM, AND—WHEN IT WAS SAFE—WE TOOK THEM INSIDE A LITTLE.

SEVERAL TIMES CAME THE JEWISH POLICE TO OUR HOUSE...

OUR RECORDS SHOW THAT MR. AND MRS. KARMIO LIVE HERE. THEY HAVEN'T REGISTERED FOR TRANSFER.

YES - MY WIFE'S PARENTS - THEY LEFT WITHOUT A WORD A MONTH AGO.

JEWISH POLICE?

YES - WITH BIG STICKS.

SOME JEWS THOUGHT IN THIS WAY: IF THEY GAVE TO THE GERMANS A FEW JEWS, THEY COULD SAVE THE REST.

AND AT LEAST THEY COULD SAVE THEMSELVES.

AND A MONTH AFTER, THEY AGAIN CAME TO FATHER-IN-LAW.

MR. ZYLBERBERG, YOU AND YOUR WIFE MUST COME WITH US.

IF THE KARMIOS DON'T TURN UP IN 3 DAYS YOU TWO WILL BE SENT IN THEIR PLACE!

HE HAD STILL A LITTLE "PROTECTION" FROM THE GEMEINDE, SO THEY TOOK ONLY HIM AWAY-NOT HIS WIFE.

HE SAT A FEW DAYS THERE, THEN HE SENT TO US A NOTE

HE WROTE THAT WE HAD TO GIVE OVER THE GRANDPARENTS. EVEN IF THEY TOOK ONLY HIM AWAY NOW, NEXT THEY WOULD GRAB HIS WIFE, AND THEN THE REST OF THE FAMILY.

SO, WHAT HAPPENED?

WHAT HAPPENED? WE HAD TO DELIVER THEM!

THEY THOUGHT IT WAS TO THERESIENSTADT THEY WERE GOING.

LET US KNOW IF YOU NEED ANYTHING!

BUT THEY WENT RIGHT AWAY TO AUSCHWITZ, TO THE GAS.

WHEN DID YOU FIRST HEAR ABOUT AUSCHWITZ?

RIGHT **AWAY** WE HEARD...

EVEN FROM THERE - FROM THAT OTHER WORLD-PEOPLE CAME BACK AND TOLD US. BUT WE DIDN'T BELIEVE.

THEN THIS SAME NEWS CAME MORE AND MORE, SO WE BELIEVED. AND LATER ON, WE **SAW** ..." EVEN **WORSE**!

AFTER WHAT HAPPENED TO THE GRANDPARENTS, IT WAS A FEW MONTHS QUIET. THEN IT CAME POSTERS EVERYWHERE AND SPEECHES FROM THE GEMEINDE...

FELLOW JEWS: ON WEDNESDAY, AUGUST 12TH, EVERY ONE OF YOU, YOUNG AND OLD, MALE AND FEMALE, HEALTHY AND SICK, MUST REGISTER AT THE *DIENST* STADIUM...

OH NO!

NOW WHAT?

...THERE'S NO CAUSE FOR ALARM-IT'S ONLY A MATTER OF INSPECTING YOUR DOCUMENTS AND STAMPING THEM. THIS WILL PROTECT YOU AS CITIZENS OF THE REGION!...

I'M NOT GOING. IT'S A NAZI TRAP!...

EVERYBODY WAS WORRIED.

...AND OUR JEWISH COMMITTEE IS **HELPING** THOSE MURDERERS. GOD KNOWS WHAT WILL HAPPEN TO US AT THE STADIUM!

WELL, THEY JUST INSPECTED JEWISH DOCUMENTS IN SOME NEARBY TOWNS. IT WAS NO BIG DEAL.

ANYWAY, WE'VE **GOT** TO GO. WITHOUT LEGAL PAPERS, WE'RE LOST!

TO GO, IT WAS NO GOOD. BUT, NOT TO GO — IT WAS ALSO NO GOOD.

MY FATHER-HE HAD 62 YEARS-CAME BY STREETCAR TO ME FROM DABROWA, THE VILLAGE NEXT DOOR FROM SOSNOWIEC.

AFTER MY MOTHER DIED WITH CANCER, HE LIVED THERE IN THE HOUSE OF MY SISTER FELA, AND HER FOUR SMALL CHILDREN.

HERE'S A COOKIE, RICHIEU. AUNT FELA BAKED IT FOR YOU.

SAY THANK YOU TO GRANDPA.

I NEED YOUR ADVICE, VLADEK. SHOULD I GO TO THE STADIUM ON WEDNESDAY, OR HIDE AT HOME?

I DON'T KNOW. I'M NOT EVEN SURE WHAT WE'RE GOING TO DO. ...ANJA'S MOTHER SAYS SHE ISN'T GO-ING. SHE'S SICK AND AFRAID.

AT LEAST ANJA'S FATHER, LOLEK AND I ALL WORK AT THE GERMAN WOODSHOP. WE'RE A LITTLE SAFER. BUT YOU DON'T WORK. YOU HAVE NO PAPERS. YOU DON'T HAVE ANYTHING!

WELL, OUR COUSIN MORDECAI SAYS HE'LL BE AT ONE OF THE INSPECTION TABLES. I COULD BRING MY PAPERS TO HIM...

WHAT DOES FELA SAY?

SHE'S NOT SURE...BUT IF FELA DECIDES TO GO, OF COURSE I'LL GO WITH HER.

CAN I HAVE ANOTHER COOKIE?

RICHIEU!

REALLY, I DIDN'T KNOW HOW TO ADVISE HIM.

BUT FINALLY HE DID GO. PEOPLE WERE AFRAID TO NOT SHOW UP.

SO IT CAME TO THE STADIUM ALMOST ALL THE JEWS OF SOSNOWIEC, AND FROM THE OTHER VILLAGES NEAR, MAYBE 25 OR 30,000 PEOPLE.

EVERYONE CAME VERY NICE DRESSED. THEY TRIED SO THAT THEY WOULD LOOK YOUNG AND ABLE TO WORK, IN ORDER TO GET A GOOD STAMP ON THEIR PASSPORT.

WHEN WE WERE EVERYBODY INSIDE, GESTAPO WITH MACHINE GUNS SURROUNDED THE STADIUM.

LINE UP BY FAMILY AT THE TABLES TO REGISTER! QUICKLY!

THEN WAS A SELECTION, WITH PEOPLE SENT EITHER TO THE LEFT, EITHER TO THE RIGHT.

OLD PEOPLE, FAMILIES WITH LOTS OF KIDS, AND PEOPLE WITHOUT WORK CARDS ARE ALL GOING TO THE LEFT!

WE UNDERSTOOD THIS MUST BE VERY BAD.

ME AND ANJA CAME TO THE TABLE WHERE MY COUSIN WAS SITTING...

AH, YOU WORK AT THE CARPENTRY SHOP.. GO TO THE RIGHT.

SO WE GOT STAMPED OUR PASSPORTS AND CAME QUICK TO THE GOOD SIDE OF THE STADIUM. THOSE THEY SENT LEFT, THEY DIDN'T GET ANY STAMP.

WE WERE SO HAPPY WE CAME THROUGH. BUT WE WORRIED NOW— WERE OUR FAMILIES SAFE?

LOOK! THERE'S POPPA, WITH LOLEK AND LONIA!

WE SAW WOLFE AND TOSHA. OUR FAMILY SEEMS TO BE OKAY.

DID YOU SEE MY FATHER?

I COULDN'T SEE ANYWHERE MY FATHER.

BUT LATER SOMEONE WHO SAW HIM TOLD ME... HE CAME THROUGH THIS SAME COUSIN OVER TO THE GOOD SIDE.

SPIEGELMAN... TO THE RIGHT.

THEN CAME FELA TO REGISTER...

HER, THEY SENT TO THE LEFT. FOUR CHILDREN WAS TOO MANY.

FELA!

MY DAUGHTER! HOW CAN SHE MANAGE ALONE—WITH FOUR CHILDREN TO TAKE CARE OF?

AND, WHAT DO YOU THINK? HE SNEAKED ON TO THE BAD SIDE!

AND THOSE ON THE BAD SIDE NEVER CAME ANYMORE HOME.

THOSE WITH A STAMP WERE LET TO GO HOME. BUT THERE WERE VERY FEW JEWS NOW LEFT IN SOSNOWIEC...

ONE FROM THREE THEY KEPT AT THE STADIUM.... MAYBE 10,000 PEOPLE—AND WITH THEM, MY FATHER.

WELL....IT'S ENOUGH FOR TODAY. YES, ARTIE?...

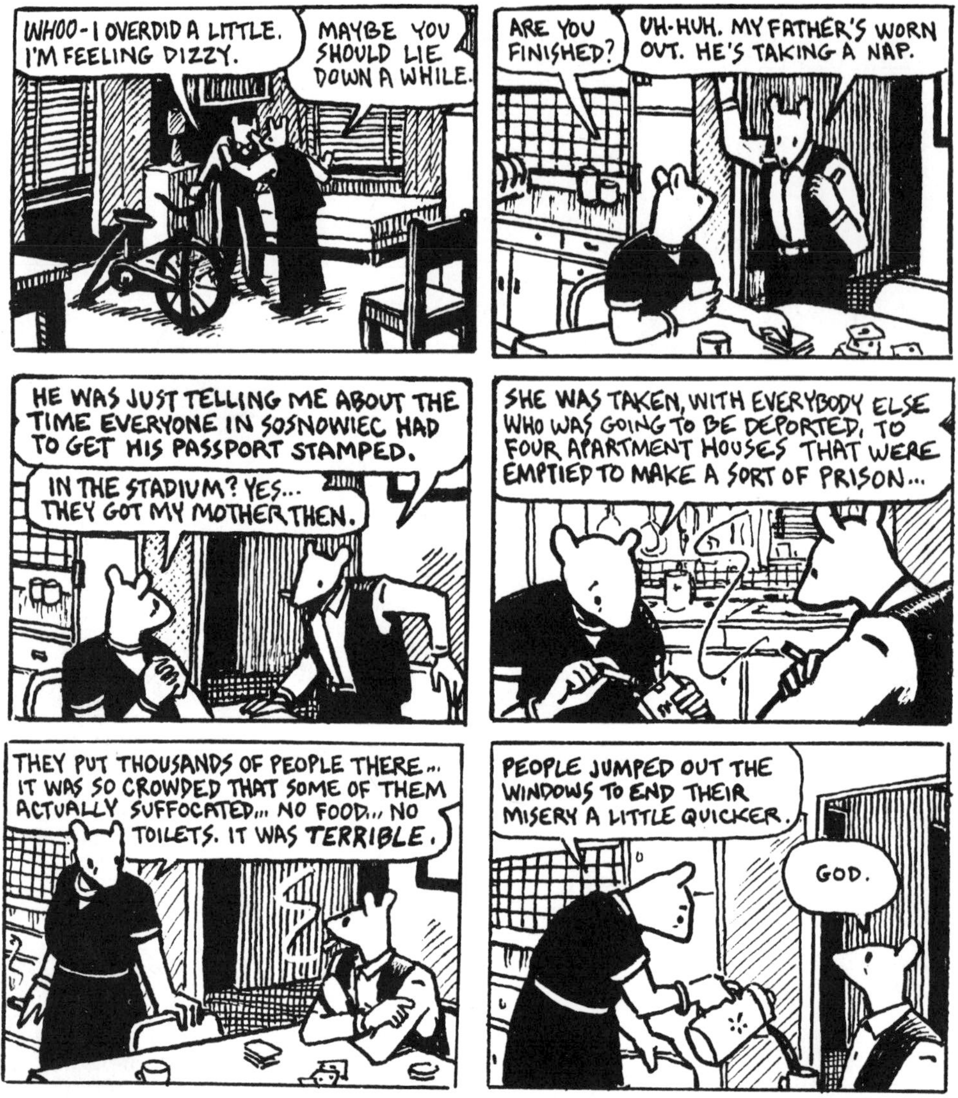
WHOO-I OVERDID A LITTLE. I'M FEELING DIZZY.
MAYBE YOU SHOULD LIE DOWN A WHILE.
ARE YOU FINISHED?
UH-HUH. MY FATHER'S WORN OUT. HE'S TAKING A NAP.
HE WAS JUST TELLING ME ABOUT THE TIME EVERYONE IN SOSNOWIEC HAD TO GET HIS PASSPORT STAMPED.
IN THE STADIUM? YES... THEY GOT MY MOTHER THEN.
SHE WAS TAKEN, WITH EVERYBODY ELSE WHO WAS GOING TO BE DEPORTED, TO FOUR APARTMENT HOUSES THAT WERE EMPTIED TO MAKE A SORT OF PRISON...
THEY PUT THOUSANDS OF PEOPLE THERE... IT WAS SO CROWDED THAT SOME OF THEM ACTUALLY SUFFOCATED... NO FOOD... NO TOILETS. IT WAS *TERRIBLE*.
PEOPLE JUMPED OUT THE WINDOWS TO END THEIR MISERY A LITTLE QUICKER.
GOD.
BUT MY MOTHER *SURVIVED* THAT. HER BROTHER WAS ON THE JEWISH COMMITTEE, AND HE HID HER IN A COAL CELLAR 'TIL ALL THE TRANSPORTS LEFT.
THEN HE GOT ME A JOB SCRUBBING THE PEOPLE'S FILTH — *VOMIT! EXCREMENT!* — OUT OF SEVERAL APARTMENTS, AND I MANAGED TO SMUGGLE HER OUT.

EVENTUALLY SHE AND MY FATHER BOTH ENDED UP IN AUSCHWITZ. THEY DIED THERE.

WHERE ARE YOU GOING? YOU DIDN'T DRINK YOUR COFFEE.

I JUST THOUGHT OF SOMETHING. MY FATHER MENTIONED THAT ANJA USED TO KEEP A DIARY, AND I *VAGUELY* REMEMBER SEEING THEM ON HIS SHELVES IN THE DEN.

I DOUBT IT. I WOULD HAVE NOTICED THEM.

WELL, THERE'S SO MUCH JUNK IN THERE, IT'S WORTH A SHOT.

LOOK AT ALL THIS STUFF! ...OLD MENUS HE PICKED UP ON CRUISES. ...A PILE OF STATIONERY FROM THE PINES HOTEL...

INCREDIBLE! FOUR 1965 DRY DOCK SAVINGS BANK CALENDARS...I'LL BET HE NEVER EVEN HAD AN ACCOUNT THERE.

HE DRIVES ME CRAZY! HE WON'T EVEN LET ME THROW OUT THE PLASTIC PITCHER HE TOOK FROM HIS HOSPITAL ROOM LAST YEAR!

HE'S MORE ATTACHED TO THINGS THAN TO PEOPLE!

I REALLY DON'T KNOW HOW LONG I CAN TAKE HIM. I REALLY DON'T.

I BETTER BE GETTING HOME. I'LL LOOK FOR THOSE DIARIES NEXT TIME.

WAIT! PUT EVERYTHING BACK EXACTLY LIKE IT WAS, OR I'LL NEVER HEAR THE END OF IT!

OKAY... OKAY... RELAX.

# CHAPTER FIVE

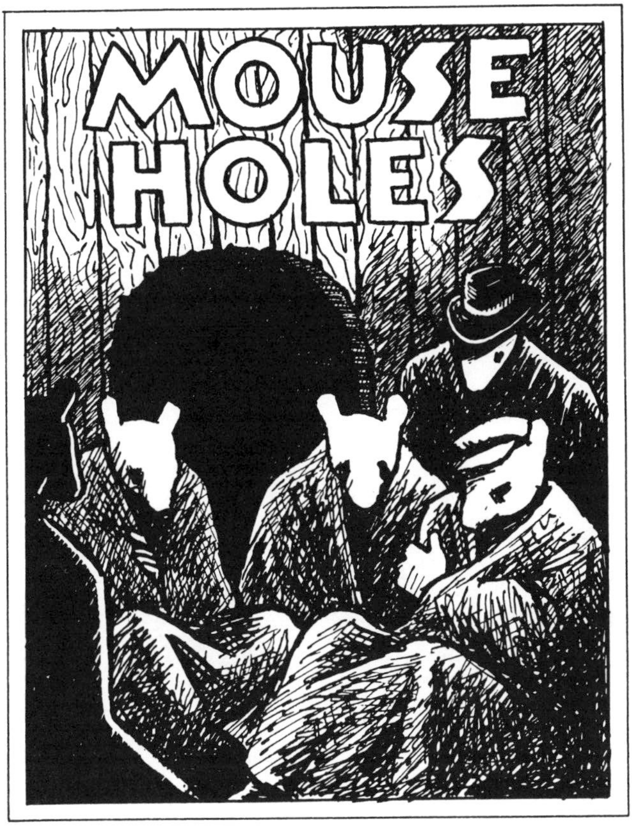
MOUSE
HOLES

MNF?

HELLO, ARTIE? I'M TELLING YOU, I DON'T KNOW WHAT TO DO WITH YOUR FATHER—HE JUST CLIMBED ONTO THE ROOF!..

UNH? MALA?

HE INSISTED ON FIXING THE DRAIN-PIPE AND GOT DIZZY! I DON'T KNOW HOW I EVER GOT HIM DOWN!

WHAT TIME IS IT?

NOW HE WANTS TO CLIMB BACK UP! WHAT AM I SUPPOSED TO DO?!

PLEASE DON'T SHOUT.

WHY DON'T YOU CALL A *HANDYMAN*? JEEZ, MALA, IT'S ONLY 7:30 AM. FRANÇOISE AND I WERE UP 'TIL 4:00! YOU *KNOW* WE DON'T GET UP 'TIL—

HELLO? ARTIE? IT'S *POPPA* HERE.

I'M TELLING YOU, MALA MAKES ME *MESHUGAH!* I WANT THAT MAYBE *YOU* COULD COME NOW TO QUEENS TO HELP ME.

WHAT? YOU'VE GOTTA BE KIDDING!

WHEN I WAS YOUNG I COULD DO BY MY-SELF THESE THINGS. BUT NOW, DARLING I NEED IT YOUR HELP FOR THE DRAINPIPE!

UM-LOOK, POP. I'LL CALL YOU BACK AFTER I'VE HAD SOME COFFEE.

WHEW. MAYBE I WAS DREAMING.

WUZZIT? YOUR FATHER AGAIN?

96

UH-HUH. HE WANTS ME TO GO HELP HIM FIX HIS ROOF OR SOMETHING. *SHIT!* EVEN AS A KID I HATED HELPING HIM AROUND THE HOUSE.

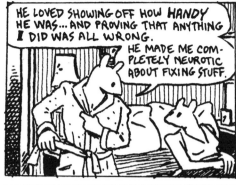

HE LOVED SHOWING OFF HOW *HANDY* HE WAS... AND PROVING THAT ANYTHING *I* DID WAS ALL WRONG.

HE MADE ME COMPLETELY NEUROTIC ABOUT FIXING STUFF.

I MEAN, I DIDN'T EVEN OWN A *HAMMER* BEFORE WE MOVED INTO THIS PLACE!

ONE REASON I BECAME AN ARTIST WAS THAT HE THOUGHT IT WAS IMPRACTICAL—JUST A WASTE OF TIME ...

...IT WAS AN AREA WHERE I WOULDN'T HAVE TO COMPETE WITH HIM.

SO... ARE YOU GOING OUT TO QUEENS?

NO WAY—I'D RATHER FEEL GUILTY! BESIDES, I'M TOO BUSY, AND HE CAN EASILY AFFORD TO HIRE SOMEBODY.

UH, HELLO POP. LISTEN... ABOUT THAT DRAINPIPE... I DON'T THINK I CAN COME. I—

SO? NEVER MIND ARTIE...

I TALKED JUST NOW TO FRANK, WHAT LIVES NEXT DOOR. HE AGREED HE WOULD FIX WITH ME OVER THE WEEKEND.

THAT'S GREAT!

YES. OF COURSE, BETTER IT WOULD BE FIXED TODAY—BUT AT LEAST *SOMEBODY* WILL HELP ME!

JUST GREAT.

About a week later, early afternoon...

HIYA, POP. WHATCHA DOING OUT HERE IN THE GARAGE?

IT'S ALWAYS **SOMETHING** HERE I MUST DO. I'M PUTTING NOW AWAY MY OLD NAILS — THE LONG ONES SEPARATE FROM THE SHORT ONES.

PLINK

IS THE ROOF ALL FIXED UP?

YAH- FRANK FROM NEXT DOOR CAME EVENTUALLY AND TOGETHER WE FIXED.

UM... DO YOU NEED ANY HELP WITH THOSE NAILS OR ANYTHING?

NO....

SUCH JOBS I CAN DO EASY BY MYSELF.

PLUNK

UM... IS EVERY-THING OKAY?

PLINK

NU? WITH MY LIFE NOW, YOU KNOW IT **CAN'T** BE EVERYTHING OKAY!

YOU GO UPSTAIRS. I'LL FINISH HERE MY JOB, AND IN A FEW MINUTES I'LL COME UP.

OKAY.

PLINK

HI, MALA.

OY! YOU SCARED ME, ARTIE. MY NERVES ARE COMPLETELY SHOT, LIVING WITH YOUR FATHER.

HE SEEMED A LITTLE UPSET WHEN I SAW HIM DOWNSTAIRS... DO YOU THINK HE'S ANGRY THAT I DIDN'T COME HELP HIM LAST WEEK?

I DON'T THINK SO..

BUT KEEPING THIS HOUSE FIXED UP IS TOO MUCH FOR HIM NOW. I KEEP TELLING HIM TO SELL IT AND BUY A CONDO IN MIAMI.

HE SEEMS DEPRESSED.

IT COULD BE THAT COMIC STRIP YOU ONCE MADE – THE ONE ABOUT YOUR MOTHER.

WHAT?

VLADEK SAW IT FOR THE FIRST TIME A COUPLE OF DAYS AGO.

HOW DO YOU KNOW ABOUT "PRISONER ON THE HELL PLANET"?

MY FRIEND, RUTHIE, HAS A SON IN COLLEGE. HE READS ALL THE COMICS. HE SHOWED IT TO HER, AND SHE GAVE ME A COPY.

SHIT!...

I KNEW IT WOULD UPSET YOUR FATHER, SO I KEPT IT HIDDEN. BUT, SOMEHOW HE FOUND IT.

I DREW THIS STORY YEARS AGO.

IT APPEARED IN AN OBSCURE UNDERGROUND COMIC BOOK. I NEVER THOUGHT VLADEK WOULD SEE IT.

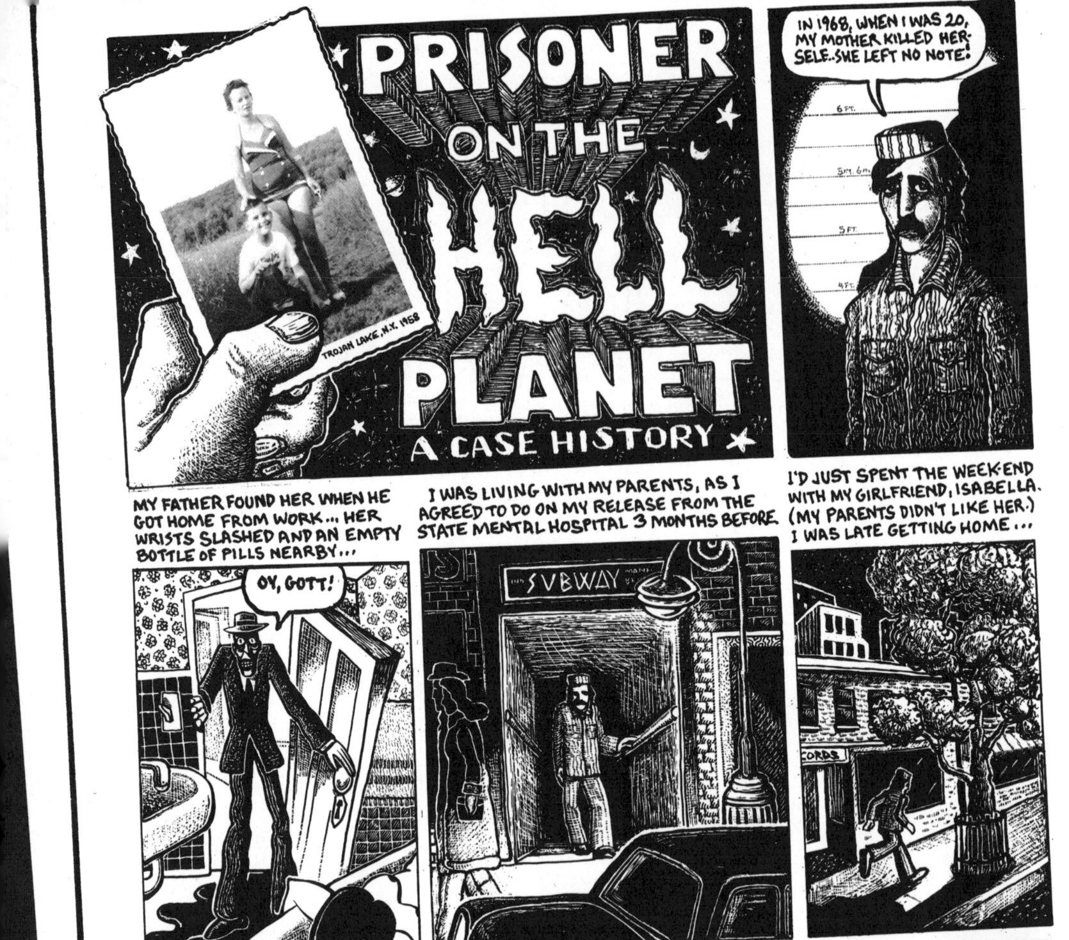
PRISONER ON THE HELL PLANET
A CASE HISTORY
TROJAN LAKE, N.Y. 1958
IN 1968, WHEN I WAS 20, MY MOTHER KILLED HER-SELF..SHE LEFT NO NOTE!
6 FT.
5 FT. 6 IN.
5 FT.
4 FT.
MY FATHER FOUND HER WHEN HE GOT HOME FROM WORK... HER WRISTS SLASHED AND AN EMPTY BOTTLE OF PILLS NEARBY...
OY, GOTT!
I WAS LIVING WITH MY PARENTS, AS I AGREED TO DO ON MY RELEASE FROM THE STATE MENTAL HOSPITAL 3 MONTHS BEFORE.
SUBWAY
I'D JUST SPENT THE WEEK-END WITH MY GIRLFRIEND, ISABELLA. (MY PARENTS DIDN'T LIKE HER.) I WAS LATE GETTING HOME...
CORDS
I SUPPOSE THAT IF I'D GOTTEN HOME WHEN EXPECTED, I WOULD HAVE FOUND HER BODY...
63-12
WHEN I SAW THE CROWD I HAD A PANG OF FEAR... I SUSPECTED THE WORST, BUT DIDN'T LET MYSELF KNOW!

A COUSIN HERDED ME AWAY FROM THE SCENE.

COME TO THE DOCTOR'S.... YOUR MOTHER IS -AH- SICK!... HE WILL EXPLAIN ......

DOCTOR ORENS LIVED NEARBY...

SIT DOWN, ARTHUR... I THOUGHT I SHOULD BE THE ONE TO TELL YOU...

YOUR MOTHER KILLED HERSELF—SHE'S DEAD!

I COULD AVOID THE TRUTH NO LONGER—THE DOCTOR'S WORDS CLATTERED INSIDE ME.... I FELT CONFUSED, I FELT ANGRY, I FELT NUMB!... I DIDN'T EXACTLY FEEL LIKE CRYING, BUT FIGURED I SHOULD!....

SHE'S DEAD! A SUICIDE!

NOW, NOW, BOY...

NO, LET HIM CRY— IT'S GOOD FOR HIM!

WE WENT HOME... MY FATHER HAD COMPLETELY FALLEN APART!...

OY, ARTIE! WHY? WHY! SUCH A TRAGEDY! AND NOT EVEN A NOTE!!!

I WAS EXPECTED TO COMFORT HIM!

MOTHER... MOTHER...

SOMEHOW THE FUNERAL ARRANGEMENTS WERE MADE...

...AND FOR $950.00 WE HAVE A BRONZE CASKET WITH BRONZE-COLORED VELVET— OF COURSE, FOR $2,000.00 WE CAN...

PROTECT WHAT YOU HAVE

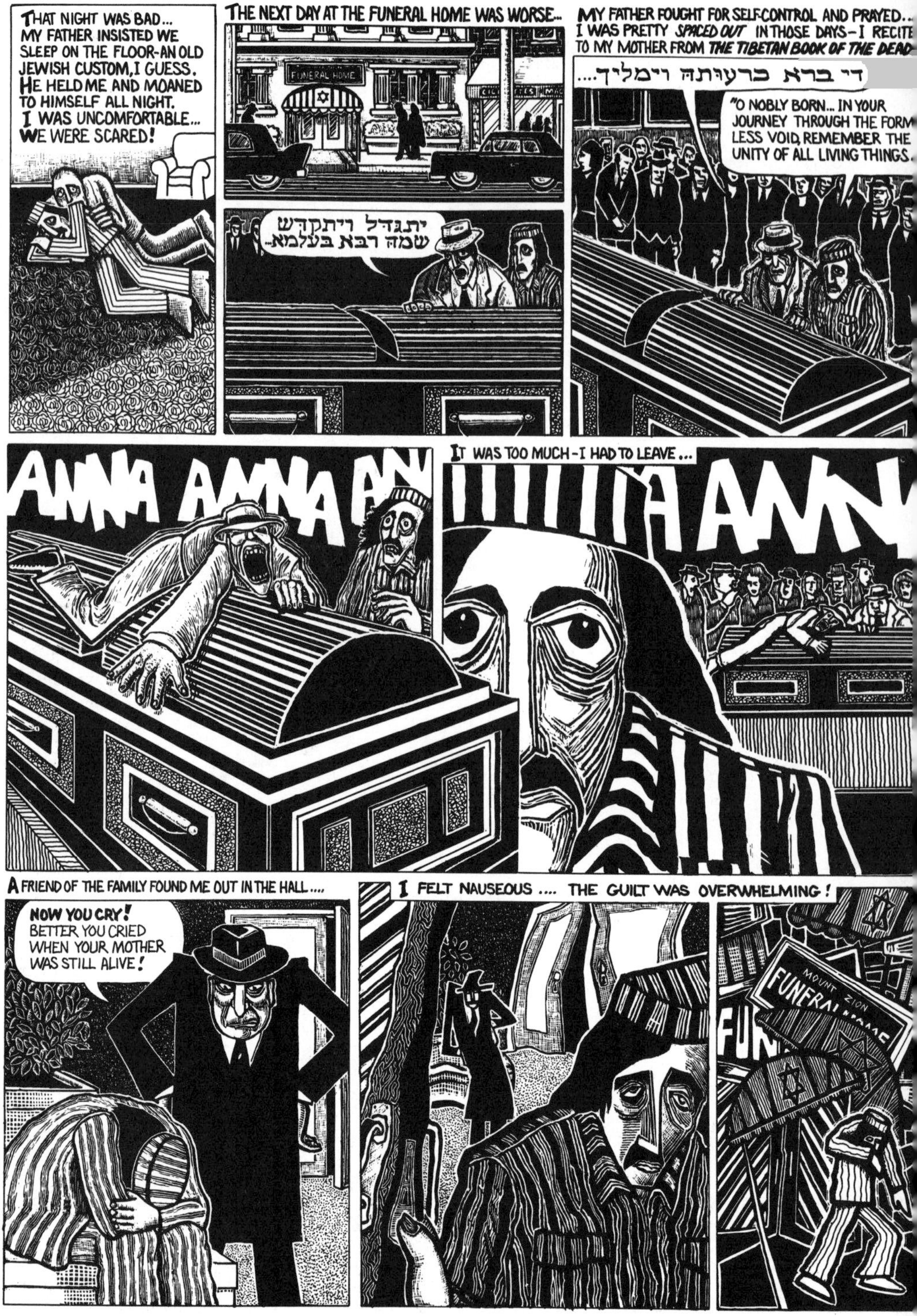
THAT NIGHT WAS BAD... MY FATHER INSISTED WE SLEEP ON THE FLOOR-AN OLD JEWISH CUSTOM, I GUESS. HE HELD ME AND MOANED TO HIMSELF ALL NIGHT. I WAS UNCOMFORTABLE... WE WERE SCARED!
THE NEXT DAY AT THE FUNERAL HOME WAS WORSE...
FUNERAL HOME
יתגדל ויתקדש
שמה רבא בעלמא.
MY FATHER FOUGHT FOR SELF-CONTROL AND PRAYED.. I WAS PRETTY *SPACED OUT* IN THOSE DAYS-I RECITE TO MY MOTHER FROM *THE TIBETAN BOOK OF THE DEAD*
די ברא כרעותה וימליך....
"O NOBLY BORN... IN YOUR JOURNEY THROUGH THE FORMLESS VOID, REMEMBER THE UNITY OF ALL LIVING THINGS."
ANNA ANNA ANN
IT WAS TOO MUCH-I HAD TO LEAVE...
IIIIIIA ANN
A FRIEND OF THE FAMILY FOUND ME OUT IN THE HALL....
NOW YOU CRY! BETTER YOU CRIED WHEN YOUR MOTHER WAS STILL ALIVE!
I FELT NAUSEOUS .... THE GUILT WAS OVERWHELMING!
MOUNT ZION
FUNERAL HOME
FUN

THE NEXT WEEK WE SPENT IN MOURNING... MY FATHER'S FRIENDS ALL OFFERED ME HOSTILITY MIXED IN WITH THEIR CONDOLENCES...

ARTHUR—WE'RE *SO* SORRY...

IT'S HIS FAULT— THE PUNK!

THEY THINK IT'S MY FAULT!!

...BUT, FOR THE MOST PART, I WAS LEFT ALONE WITH MY THOUGHTS...

MENOPAUSAL DEPRESSION
HITLER DID IT!
MOMMY!
BITCH

I REMEMBERED THE LAST TIME I SAW HER—

...ARTIE...

SHE CAME INTO MY ROOM... IT WAS LATE AT NIGHT....

...ARTIE ... YOU... STILL... LOVE... ME ..., DON'T YOU? ....

...I TURNED AWAY, RESENTFUL OF THE WAY SHE TIGHTENED THE UMBILICAL CORD...

SURE, MA!

...SHE WALKED OUT AND CLOSED THE DOOR!

CLIK!

AGH!

WELL, MOM, IF YOU'RE LISTENING...

CONGRATULATIONS!... YOU'VE COMMITTED THE PERFECT CRIME ....

...YOU PUT ME HERE .... SHORTED ALL MY CIRCUITS...CUT MY NERVE ENDINGS ... AND CROSSED MY WIRES!....

...YOU *MURDERED* ME, MOMMY, AND YOU LEFT ME HERE TO TAKE THE RAP!!!

PIPE DOWN, MAC! SOME OF US ARE TRYING TO SLEEP!

© art spiegelman, 1972

GEE, I'M SURPRISED THAT VLADEK *READ* THIS WHEN HE FOUND IT. HE *NEVER* READS COMICS...

HE DOESN'T EVEN LOOK AT MY WORK WHEN I STICK IT UNDER HIS NOSE.

BUT THIS ISN'T *LIKE* OTHER COMICS...

I TELL YOU, WHEN RUTHIE SHOWED IT TO ME I THOUGHT I'D *FAINT.* I WAS SO SHOCKED.

IT WAS SO... SO *PERSONAL!*

...BUT VERY ACCURATE.... OBJECTIVE. I SPENT A LOT OF TIME HELPING OUT HERE AFTER ANJA'S FUNERAL. IT WAS JUST AS YOU SAID.

SO, ARTIE. I'M READY.

LET'S WALK NOW TO THE BANK TOGETHER.

MALA JUST TOLD ME THAT YOU SAW MY COMIC ...THE ONE ABOUT MOM.

YES. I FOUND IT WHEN I LOOKED FOR THE THINGS YOU ASKED ME LAST TIME. HOO! I SAW THE PICTURE THERE OF MOM, SO I READ IT... AND I CRIED.

I-I'M SORRY.

IT'S GOOD YOU GOT IT OUTSIDE YOUR SYSTEM. BUT FOR ME IT BROUGHT IN MY MIND SO MUCH *MEMORIES* OF ANJA.

...OF COURSE I'M THINKING ALWAYS ABOUT HER *ANYWAY.*

YES. YOU KEEP PHOTOS OF HER ALL AROUND YOUR DESK–LIKE A SHRINE!

WHAT HAVE I TO DO, MALA? IN THE GARBAGE PUT THEM? OF YOU *ALSO* I HAVE A PHOTO ON THE DESK!

ACH! DON'T DO ME ANY FAVORS!

YOU SEE WHAT I HAVE WITH HER? ALWAYS, WHATEVER I DO IS NO GOOD.

DID YOU FIND MOM'S DIARY?

SO FAR THIS DIDN'T SHOW UP. I LOOKED, BUT I CAN'T FIND.

I'VE **GOT** TO HAVE THAT!

ANOTHER TIME I'LL AGAIN LOOK. BUT NOW BETTER WE GO TO THE BANK.

OKAY.

..EVERY DAY I WALK, OTHERWISE IN MY LEGS THE CIRCULATION MAKES ME A CRAMP. IT'S SOMETHING TERRIBLE AND I CAN'T SLEEP.

BUT FOR MY HEART, I MUST WALK SLOW.

WHAT HAPPENED TO YOU AND ANJA AFTER THE BIG SELECTION AT THE STADIUM?

WELL, FOR A TIME IT WAS EVERYTHING QUIET. THEN IN 1943 CAME AN ORDER: ALL JEWS WHAT ARE LEFT IN SOSNOWIEC MUST GO TO LIVE IN AN OLD VILLAGE NEARBY CALLED SRODULA.

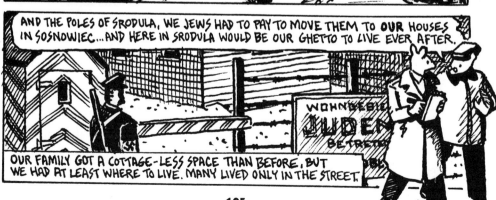

AND THE POLES OF SRODULA, WE JEWS HAD TO PAY TO MOVE THEM TO **OUR** HOUSES IN SOSNOWIEC... AND HERE IN SRODULA WOULD BE OUR GHETTO TO LIVE EVER AFTER.

WOHNGEBIE
JUDE
BETRET

OUR FAMILY GOT A COTTAGE-LESS SPACE THAN BEFORE, BUT WE HAD AT LEAST WHERE TO LIVE. MANY LIVED ONLY IN THE STREET.

EACH DAY WE WERE TAKEN TO SOSNOWIEC, TO WORK IN GERMAN "SHOPS"...

ANJA, WITH HER SISTER, TOSHA, THEY WORKED IN A CLOTHINGS FACTORY...

AND I WENT, TOGETHER WITH MY NEPHEW, LOLEK, TO A WOODWORK SHOP.

EVERY DAY THE GUARDS MARCHED US ABOUT AN HOUR AND A HALF TO WORK.

THE GUARDS, IT WAS JEWS WITH BIG STICKS. THEY ACTED SO, JUST LIKE THE GERMANS.

...AND EVERY NIGHT THEY MARCHED US BACK, COUNTED US, AND LOCKED US IN.

VLADEK! LOLEK! HURRY HOME!

ANJA! WHAT IS IT?

WOLFE'S UNCLE PERSIS IS AT OUR HOUSE!

FROM ZAWIERCIE?

YES. HE'S A BIG SHOT THERE...THE HEAD OF THEIR JEWISH COUNCIL. HE WANTS WOLFE, TOSHA AND BIBI TO GO LIVE WITH HIM IN ZAWIERCIE.

...YOU'VE ALL HEARD THE STORIES ABOUT AUSCHWITZ. HORRIBLE, UNBELIEVABLE STORIES.

THEY CAN'T BE TRUE!

ONE THING IS CERTAIN— AS BAD AS THINGS ARE IN THE GHETTO, BEING DEPORTED IS EVEN WORSE.

PLEASE! IT'S BAD LUCK TO EVEN SPEAK OF IT!

LOOK. YOU DON'T HAVE MUCH INFLUENCE HERE. IN ZAWIERCIE I HAVE SOME INFLUENCE WITH THE GERMANS... I CAN BRIBE THEM.

MY 90-YEAR-OLD FATHER STILL LIVES WITH ME...WHENEVER THERE'S A ROUND-UP, AN S.S. MAN GUARDS HIM TO KEEP HIM SAFE!

NINETY! THIS WAS 1943! IT WASN'T LEFT ANY OTHER JEWS WHAT HAD NINETY YEARS!

PERSIS WAS REALLY A FINE MAN—NOT SO LIKE MONIEK MERIN, THE HEAD OF OUR GHETTO, WHO LOOKED ONLY OUT FOR HIMSELF. ...PERSIS TRIED REALLY TO HELP HIS JEWS.

I CAN MANAGE PAPERS TO TAKE WOLFE, TOSHA AND BIBI—AND MAYBE LITTLE LONIA AND RICHIEU IF YOU'LL LET ME.

YES. THEY'D BE BETTER OFF.

YOU SEE? I WANTED TO SEND RICHIEU SOMEPLACE SAFE A YEAR AGO— WITH ILZECKI'S CHILD!

THINGS ARE EVEN WORSE NOW, VLADEK. WE HAVE NO CHOICE!

NO! WE MUST ALL STAY TOGETHER! WE'VE MADE IT THIS FAR. GOD WILL STILL HELP US!

MATKA! BE REALISTIC!

ANJA'S MOTHER DIDN'T LIKE TO LOOK AT THE FACTS. BUT FINALLY EVEN SHE AGREED,

 SO PERSIS ARRANGED, AND HE CAME AGAIN TO SRODULA.

IT WENT WITH HIM WOLFE, TOSHA AND BIBI

LOLEK'S LITTLE SISTER, LONIA

AND OUR BOY, RICHIEU.

WE WATCHED UNTIL THEY DISAPPEARED FROM OUR EYES...

IT WAS THE LAST TIME EVER WE SAW THEM; BUT THAT WE COULDN'T KNOW.

 WHEN THINGS CAME WORSE IN OUR GHETTO WE SAID ALWAYS: "THANK GOD THE KIDS ARE WITH PERSIS, SAFE."

 THAT SPRING, ON ONE DAY, THE GERMANS TOOK FROM SRODULA TO AUSCHWITZ OVER 1,000 PEOPLE.

MOST THEY TOOK WERE KIDS — SOME ONLY 2 OR 3 YEARS.

SOME KIDS WERE SCREAMING AND SCREAMING. THEY COULDN'T STOP.

SO THE GERMANS SWINGED THEM BY THE LEGS AGAINST A WALL...

AND THEY NEVER ANYMORE SCREAMED.

IN THIS WAY THE GERMANS TREATED THE LITTLE ONES WHAT STILL HAD SURVIVED A LITTLE.

THIS I DIDN'T SEE WITH MY OWN EYES, BUT SOMEBODY THE NEXT DAY TOLD ME. AND I SAID, "THANK GOD WITH PERSIS OUR CHILDREN ARE SAFE!"

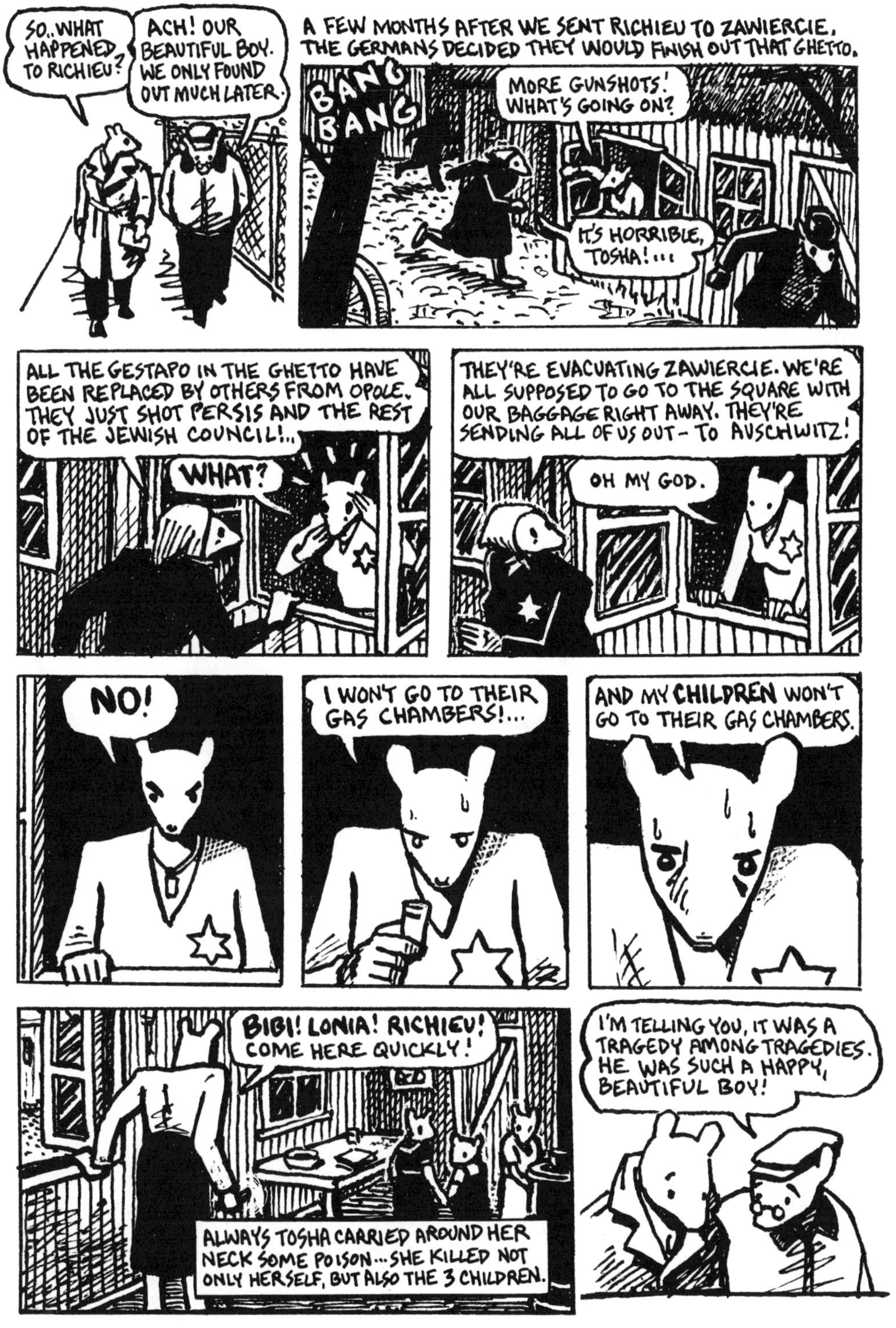

SO.. WHAT HAPPENED TO RICHIEU?
ACH! OUR BEAUTIFUL BOY. WE ONLY FOUND OUT MUCH LATER.
A FEW MONTHS AFTER WE SENT RICHIEU TO ZAWIERCIE, THE GERMANS DECIDED THEY WOULD FINISH OUT THAT GHETTO.
BANG BANG
MORE GUNSHOTS! WHAT'S GOING ON?
IT'S HORRIBLE, TOSHA!...
ALL THE GESTAPO IN THE GHETTO HAVE BEEN REPLACED BY OTHERS FROM OPOLE. THEY JUST SHOT PERSIS AND THE REST OF THE JEWISH COUNCIL!..
WHAT?
THEY'RE EVACUATING ZAWIERCIE. WE'RE ALL SUPPOSED TO GO TO THE SQUARE WITH OUR BAGGAGE RIGHT AWAY. THEY'RE SENDING ALL OF US OUT - TO AUSCHWITZ!
OH MY GOD.
NO!
I WON'T GO TO THEIR GAS CHAMBERS!...
AND MY CHILDREN WON'T GO TO THEIR GAS CHAMBERS.
BIBI! LONIA! RICHIEU! COME HERE QUICKLY!
ALWAYS TOSHA CARRIED AROUND HER NECK SOME POISON... SHE KILLED NOT ONLY HERSELF, BUT ALSO THE 3 CHILDREN.
I'M TELLING YOU, IT WAS A TRAGEDY AMONG TRAGEDIES. HE WAS SUCH A HAPPY, BEAUTIFUL BOY!

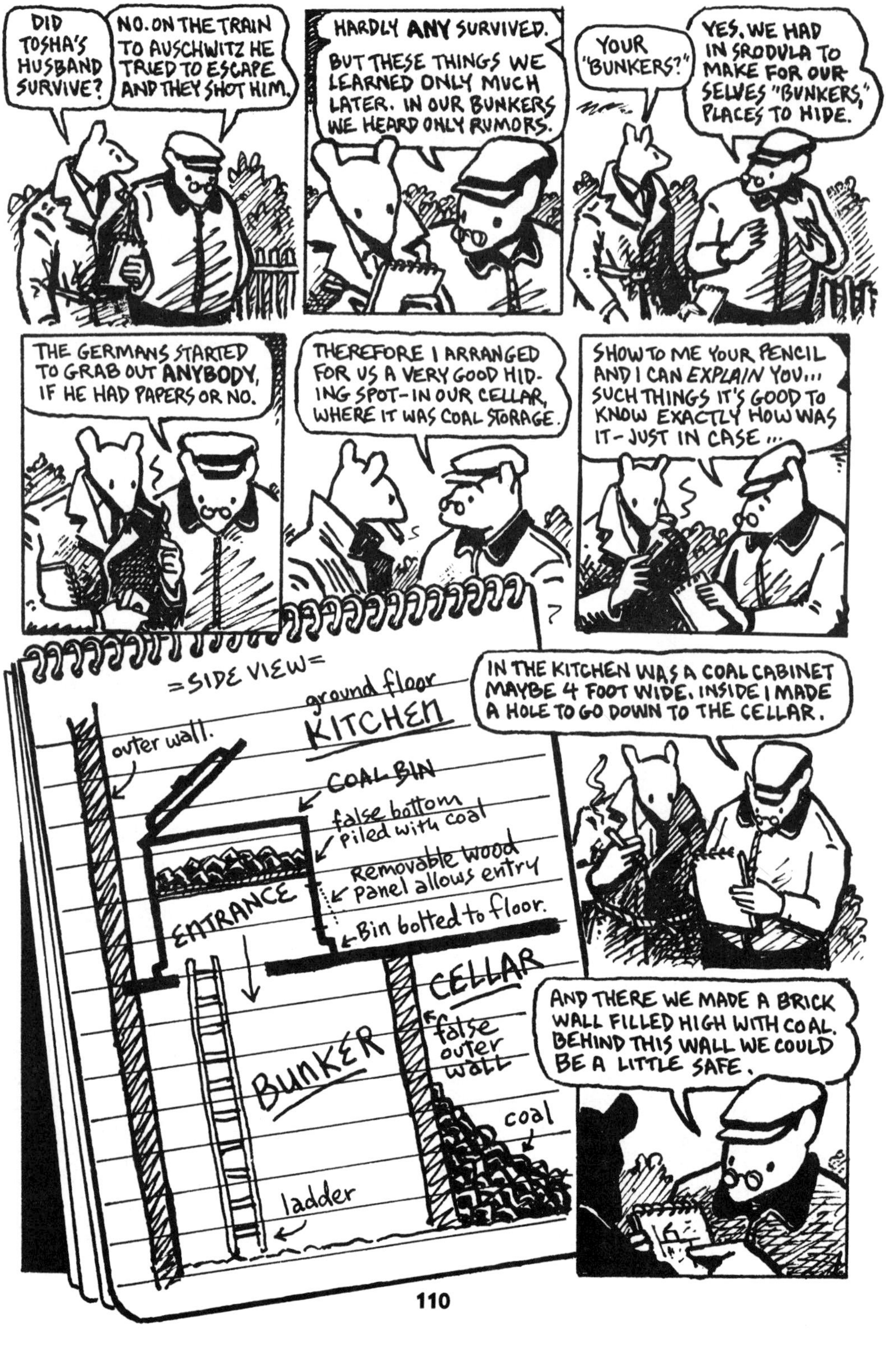
DID TOSHA'S HUSBAND SURVIVE?
NO. ON THE TRAIN TO AUSCHWITZ HE TRIED TO ESCAPE AND THEY SHOT HIM.
HARDLY ANY SURVIVED.
BUT THESE THINGS WE LEARNED ONLY MUCH LATER. IN OUR BUNKERS WE HEARD ONLY RUMORS.
YOUR "BUNKERS?"
YES. WE HAD IN SRODULA TO MAKE FOR OUR SELVES "BUNKERS," PLACES TO HIDE.
THE GERMANS STARTED TO GRAB OUT ANYBODY, IF HE HAD PAPERS OR NO.
THEREFORE I ARRANGED FOR US A VERY GOOD HIDING SPOT- IN OUR CELLAR, WHERE IT WAS COAL STORAGE.
SHOW TO ME YOUR PENCIL AND I CAN EXPLAIN YOU... SUCH THINGS IT'S GOOD TO KNOW EXACTLY HOW WAS IT- JUST IN CASE...
=SIDE VIEW=
ground floor
KITCHEN
outer wall.
COAL BIN
false bottom piled with coal
Removable wood panel allows entry
ENTRANCE
Bin bolted to floor.
CELLAR
false outer wall
BUNKER
coal
ladder
IN THE KITCHEN WAS A COAL CABINET MAYBE 4 FOOT WIDE. INSIDE I MADE A HOLE TO GO DOWN TO THE CELLAR.
AND THERE WE MADE A BRICK WALL FILLED HIGH WITH COAL. BEHIND THIS WALL WE COULD BE A LITTLE SAFE.

EVEN WHEN THEY CAME WITH **DOGS** TO SMELL US OUT—AND THEY _KNEW_ THAT JEWS ARE LAYING HERE—BUT STILL THEY COULDN'T FIND.

THE DOGS RAN UP AND DOWN LIKE MAD. BUT IN THE COAL BIN WAS ONLY COAL. IT LOOKED FULL AND THEY COULDN'T LIFT IT. AND THE CELLAR, IT WAS ONLY A CELLAR.

IS IT SAFE TO GO OUT YET? I CAN'T STAND ALL THESE WORMS CRAWLING OVER ME.

THE GERMANS ARE LEAVING!

WE HAD WORMS THERE IN THAT BUNKER.

WE'VE GOT ENOUGH FOOD TO STAY HERE A COUPLE OF DAYS. WE'D BETTER WAIT 'TIL THINGS QUIET DOWN.

WE SURVIVED THERE A FEW ACTIONS. BUT OTHERS, WHAT DIDN'T HAVE SUCH A GOOD PLACE LIKE WHAT I MADE, THEY KEPT BEING TAKEN AWAY.

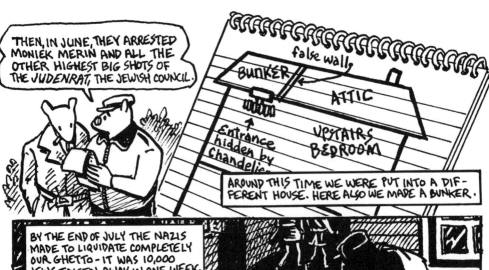

THEN, IN JUNE, THEY ARRESTED MONIEK MERIN AND ALL THE OTHER HIGHEST BIG SHOTS OF THE *JUDENRAT*, THE JEWISH COUNCIL.

false wall
BUNKER
ATTIC
UPSTAIRS BEDROOM
Entrance hidden by chandelier

AROUND THIS TIME WE WERE PUT INTO A DIFFERENT HOUSE. HERE ALSO WE MADE A BUNKER.

BY THE END OF JULY THE NAZIS MADE TO LIQUIDATE COMPLETELY OUR GHETTO - IT WAS 10,000 JEWS TAKEN AWAY IN ONE WEEK.

EXCEPT TO SNEAK FOR FOOD, WE STAYED MOSTLY IN THE BUNKER.

LOLEK! THANK GOD YOU'RE SAFE!

IT'S LIKE A BATTLEFIELD OUTSIDE!

THERE'S HARDLY ANYONE LEFT IN SRODULA. EVERYONE HAS BEEN DEPORTED OR SHOT.

FROM ALL THE JEWS OF ALL SOSNOWIEC IT WAS LEFT MAYBE 1,000 IN THE GHETTO.

AT LEAST YOUR BAG IS FULL... YOU FOUND A LOT OF FOOD, YES?

JUST A FEW OLD TURNIPS... AND SOME BOOKS.

BOOKS!? WHAT'S THE MATTER WITH YOU? WE CAN'T EAT BOOKS!

SHH

ALL THE TIME WE WERE HUNGRY. WE JUST DIDN'T HAVE WHAT TO EAT.

ONE NIGHT WE WENT TO SNEAK FOR FOOD....

LOOK! A STRANGER!

WE DRAGGED HIM UP TO OUR BUNKER

WHAT ARE YOU DOING HERE?

I-I DIDN'T KNOW ANYONE LIVED HERE! I JUST STOPPED TO REST A MOMENT.

MY WIFE AND I HAVE A STARVING BABY. I WAS OUT HUNTING FOR SCRAPS!

HE'S LYING!

HE MAY BE AN INFORMER. THE SAFEST THING WOULD BE TO KILL HIM!

WHAT HAD WE TO DO? WE TOOK ON HIM PITY.

IN THE MORNING WE GAVE A LITTLE FOOD TO HIM AND LEFT HIM GO TO HIS FAMILY....

JUDEN RAUS!

...THE GESTAPO CAME THAT AFTERNOON.

THEY TOOK US TO A BUILDING IN A PART OF SRODULA SEPARATED BY WIRES— A GHETTO INSIDE THE GHETTO—AND THERE WE HAD TO SIT AND TO WAIT.

113

WE WERE MAYBE 200 PEOPLE TOGETHER WAITING... EACH WEDNESDAY WENT VANS TO AUSCHWITZ. WHEN WE WERE CAUGHT, IT WAS THEN MAYBE A THURSDAY.

LOOK, ANJA! THAT'S MY COUSIN, JAKOV SPIEGEL-MAN, IN THE COURTYARD.

HEY! JAKOV! HELP! JAKOV-HELP US!

VLADEK?! THERE'S NOTHING I CAN DO!

I MADE SIGNS TO SHOW I COULD PAY.

SOME GOLD I HID IN THE CHIMNEY OF OUR BUNKER WHEN THEY TOOK US. BUT A FEW VALUABLES I HAD STILL WITH ME.

OKAY. DON'T WORRY! HASKEL WILL COME HELP YOU!

HASKEL SPIEGELMAN WAS ANOTHER COUSIN.

WOULDN'T THEY HAVE HELPED YOU EVEN IF YOU COULDN'T PAY? I MEAN, YOU WERE FROM THE SAME FAMILY..

HAH! YOU DON'T UNDER-STAND...

AT THAT TIME IT *WASN'T* ANYMORE FAMILIES. IT WAS EVERYBODY TO TAKE CARE FOR **HIMSELF!**

THE NEXT DAY CAME IN TWO GIRLS CARRYING FOOD. WITH THEM CAME HASKEL, A CHIEF OF THE JEWISH POLICE.

THE TWO GIRLS HE SENT BACK TO THE KITCHEN.

( LOOK, VLADEK. I CAN GET YOU AND YOUR WIFE OUT—EVEN YOUR NEPHEW. BUT YOUR IN-LAWS ARE TOO OLD. THEY'LL NEVER GET PAST THE GUARDS )

PLEASE! WE'LL MAKE IT WORTH YOUR WHILE.

QUICK, BOY. GRAB THIS EMPTY PAIL AND CARRY IT OUT WITH ME.

FROM THE WINDOW WE SAW LOLEK GO.

MY GOD, VLADEK...

YOU **MUST** GET MATKA AND ME OUT TOO. GIVE YOUR COUSIN THIS GOLD WATCH, THIS DIAMOND—ANYTHING!

OF COURSE I-I'LL DO EVERY-THING I CAN.

THE DAY AFTER, ANJA AND I CARRIED PAST THE GUARDS THE EMPTY PAILS.

HASKEL TOOK FROM ME FATHER-IN-LAW'S JEWELS. BUT, FINALLY, HE *DIDN'T* HELP THEM.

ON WEDNESDAY THE VANS CAME. ANJA AND I SAW HER FATHER AT THE WINDOW. HE WAS TEARING HIS HAIR AND CRYING.

HE WAS A MILLIONAIRE, BUT EVEN THIS DIDN'T SAVE HIM HIS LIFE.

115

SO MOM'S PARENTS DIED IN AUSCHWITZ?

NU? WHAT ELSE? RIGHT AWAY THEY WENT TO THE GAS.

HASKEL WAS HAPPY TO TAKE FROM FATHER-IN-LAW THE JEWELS—BUT THE RISK TO SAVE THEM, THIS HE WAS **NOT** SO HAPPY TO TAKE.

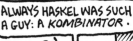

ALWAYS HASKEL WAS SUCH A GUY: A *KOMBINATOR*.

A WHAT?

A GUY WHAT MAKES *KOMBINACYA*, A SCHEMER···A CROOK.

WHAT DID YOU PICK UP?

TELEPHONE WIRE. THIS IT'S VERY HARD TO FIND.

INSIDE IT'S *LITTLE* WIRES. IT'S GOOD FOR TYING THINGS.

YOU **ALWAYS** PICK UP TRASH! CAN'T YOU JUST **BUY** WIRE?

PSSH. WHY ALWAYS YOU WANT TO **BUY** WHEN YOU CAN **FIND**!? ANYWAY, THIS WIRE THEY DON'T HAVE IT IN ANY STORES.

I'LL GIVE TO YOU SOME WIRE. YOU'LL SEE HOW USEFUL IT IS

NO THANKS! JUST TELL ME WHAT HAPPENED WITH HASKEL.

THERE ARE ONLY ABOUT A THOUSAND JEWS LEFT HERE. MOST WORK AT THE BRAUN SHOE SHOP.

HASKEL WAS A VERY BIG MAN IN THE GHETTO THEN, WHEN SRODULA WAS FINISHING.

I'LL REGISTER YOU BOTH THERE, AND —GOOD AFTERNOON, SERGEANT!

HOW ARE YOU, HERR SPIEGELMAN?

HASKEL PLAYED VERY OFTEN, CARDS WITH THE GESTAPO.

WE'LL SEE YOU TONIGHT, YES?

NATURALLY. I JUST HOPE YOU WON'T BE AS LUCKY AS LAST TIME.

HE LOST TO THEM BIG AMOUNTS OF MONEY, SO THEY WOULD LIKE HIM.

116

HASKEL HAD 2 BROTHERS, PESACH AND MILOCH. PESACH WAS ALSO A *KOMBINATOR.* BUT MILOCH, HE WAS A FINE FELLOW.

IT HAPPENED I WAS ON THE WORK DETAIL, SO.... I BURIED HIM.

HASKEL IS ALIVE STILL IN POLAND, WITH A POLISH WOMAN, A JUDGE, WHAT KEPT HIM HIDDEN WHEN **HYAAK!**

MMY HEART- ARTIE! QUICK! TAKE FROM MY POCKET A NITROSTAT PILL.

H-HERE.. YOU OKAY?

HOOSH

I-I'LL BE FINE NOW. I HAVE ONLY TO CATCH MY BREATH STILL FOR A MINUTE.

LET'S SIT ON THAT STOOP.

JUST RELAX. DON'T TALK FOR A WHILE.

HOOH! I MADE TOO FAST, OUR WALKING!

THANK GOD, WITH THE NITROSTAT IT'S COMPLETELY OVER, RIGHT AWAY! WHAT WAS I TELLING YOU?

YOU SURE YOU'RE OKAY?

WELL... YOU WERE SAYING THAT HASKEL SURVIVED THE WAR.

YES. EVEN A FEW YEARS AGO I SENT HIM PACKAGES.

GIFTS? WHY? HE SOUNDS LIKE A ROTTEN GUY!

YES. I DON'T KNOW WHY. I KNOW ONLY THAT I SENT.

YOU KNOW, ONE TIME I WAS IN THE GHETTO WALKING AROUND...

**HALT, JEW!**

GIVE ME YOUR I.D. PAPERS- I'M GOING TO BLOW YOUR BRAINS OUT,

AH. I SEE YOU'RE A MEMBER OF THE ILLUSTRIOUS SPIEGELMAN FAMILY... GO ON YOUR WAY THEN, AND GIVE HASKEL MY REGARDS.

..... *SUCH* FRIENDS HASKEL HAD,

118

I TOLD HASKEL AND MILOCH LATER ABOUT THIS.

YOU WERE VERY LUCKY, VLADEK...

THEY CALL HIM "THE SHOOTER". EVERY DAY HE KILLS SOME POOR JEW, JUST FOR FUN.

HEY! AREN'T YOU GOING OVER TO PESACH'S TO BUY SOME CAKE?

CAKE?

FOR YEARS WE DIDN'T SEE ANY CAKE. HARDLY EVEN BREAD WE SAW!

IT'S IMPOSSIBLE!

HE'S JOKING!

CAKE!

BUT COUSIN PESACH WAS REALLY SELLING CAKE! EVERYONE WHAT COULD AFFORD IT STOOD ON LINE TO BUY A PIECE...

IT LOOKS DELICIOUS.

HOW DID YOU MANAGE IT, PESACH?

WHEN PEOPLE ARE SENT TO AUSCHWITZ, MY MEN SEARCH THEIR HOUSES.

PESACH WAS LIKE HASKEL, PART OF THE JEWISH POLICE.

THEY FIND A LITTLE FLOUR HERE, A FEW GRAMS OF SUGAR THERE...I SAVED IT!

HE WAS YOUNGER FROM HASKEL, BUT ALSO A "KOMBINATOR."

YOU KNOW WHAT A COOK MY RIFKA IS... TRY IT! ONLY 75 ZLOTYS A SLICE.

I HAD STILL SAVINGS, SO I GOT FOR ANJA AND ME SOME CAKE.

BUT, THE WHOLE GHETTO, WE WERE SO SICK LATER, YOU CAN'T IMAGINE...

SOME OF THE FLOUR PESACH FOUND- IT WASN'T REALLY FLOUR, ONLY LAUNDRY SOAP, WHAT HE PUT IN THE CAKE BY MISTAKE.

OW!

GROAN

OY!

OUCH!

...WE WERE, ALL OF US, SICK LIKE DOGS.

BEFORE THE WAR PESACH HAD A RESORT HOTEL IN ZAKOPANE...

IN THOSE DAYS ALSO HE FOUND ALWAYS SCHEMES.

ALL GUESTS HAD TO PAY BIG POLISH TAXES... SO PESACH TOOK BRIBES TO NOT REGISTER THEM. BUT IF AN INSPECTOR CAME, THE GUESTS HAD TO HIDE THEMSELVES AWAY.

ONE TIME HIS WIFE MADE NOT ENOUGH DESSERTS TO GIVE TO EVERYBODY... SO PESACH RAN INTO THE DINING ROOM AND YELLED, "INSPECTORS ARE COMING!"

IT WAS NO INSPECTOR, OF COURSE. BUT 40% OF THE GUESTS RAN FAST FROM THE ROOM. ...PESACH HAD ENOUGH DESSERTS LEFT OVER EVEN FOR THE NEXT DAY!

COME.

ARE YOU READY TO WALK AGAIN?

YES, IT'S TOO *DIRTY* TO SIT! ...BUT, REALLY, IF I DIDN'T HAVE MY NITROSTAT, IT COULD HAVE BEEN JUST NOW SOMETHING TERRIBLE.

MILOCH SPIEGELMAN—HE SURVIVED THE WAR WITH HIS WIFE AND CHILD AND THEY MOVED TO AUSTRALIA. ABOUT FIVE YEARS AGO HE GOT A BIG HEART ATTACK...

AND LAST YEAR, HE GOT ON THE STREET A SEIZURE—LIKE WHAT I HAD JUST NOW... BUT HE DIDN'T HAVE WITH HIM HIS PILLS. HIS WIFE RAN TO FIND A DRUG STORE.

WHEN SHE CAME BACK MILOCH WAS DEAD!

NU? SO LIFE GOES.

BUT I MUST FINISH QUICK TO TELL YOU THE REST ABOUT SRODULA, BECAUSE WE WILL COME SOON OVER TO THE BANK.

SALE

BY THE END OF 1943 THE VANS WENT EVERY WEDNESDAY WITH MORE AND MORE AND MORE PEOPLE FROM SRODULA TO AUSCHWITZ UNTIL IT WAS VERY FEW LEFT.

IT COULD BE OUR TURN SOON, EH VLADEK?

LET'S HOPE NOT, MILOCH.

HASKEL HEARD THAT ANY DAY NOW THEY INTEND TO DEPORT EVERYONE THAT'S STILL LEFT HERE.

MILOCH TOOK ME TO THE SHOE SHOP

IT WAS EARLY AND NOBODY WAS THERE...

HASKEL MADE PLANS TO SMUGGLE HIMSELF OUT OF THE GHETTO.

PESACH AND I HAVE A PLAN ALSO...

HE MOVED A FEW SHOES FROM A PILE HIGH TO THE CEILING...

...AND TOOK ME INSIDE A TUNNEL...

DON'T TELL ANYONE ABOUT THIS EXCEPT ANJA AND YOUR NEPHEW.

...A TUNNEL MADE FROM SHOES!

WE CAME OUT TO A BUNKER...

BE PREPARED TO BRING THEM ON A MOMENT'S NOTICE!

INCREDIBLE!

EVERYTHING WAS READY HERE SO 15 OR 16 PEOPLE COULD HIDE.

...BUT WHEN ANJA AND I APPROACHED TO DISCUSS THIS BUNKER WITH LOLEK...

NO THANKS, FORGET IT!

BUT MILOCH ORGANIZED EVERYTHING!

I'M **SICK** OF HIDING!

OUR NEPHEW WAS THEN ONLY 15. HE WAS WORKING AS AN ELECTRICIAN.

ALWAYS LOLEK WAS A LITTLE MESHUGA...

I'M A SKILLED WORKER. WHEREVER THEY TAKE ME, I'LL BE OKAY.

YOU'RE CRAZY! YOU'RE GOING STRAIGHT TO THE OVENS!

AND HE *DID* GET PUT INTO ONE OF THE NEXT TRANSPORTS TO AUSCHWITZ.

ANJA BECAME COMPLETELY HYSTERICAL.

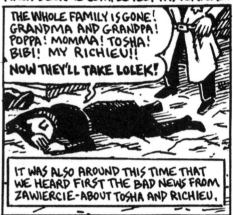

THE WHOLE FAMILY IS GONE! GRANDMA AND GRANDPA! POPPA! MOMMA! TOSHA! BIBI! MY RICHIEU!! **NOW THEY'LL TAKE LOLEK!**

IT WAS ALSO AROUND THIS TIME THAT WE HEARD FIRST THE BAD NEWS FROM ZAWIERCIE-ABOUT TOSHA AND RICHIEU.

OH GOD. LET ME DIE TOO!

COME, ANJA. GET UP!

WHY ARE YOU PULLING ME, VLADEK? LET ME ALONE! I DON'T WANT TO LIVE!

NO, DARLING! TO DIE, IT'S EASY...

BUT YOU HAVE TO *STRUGGLE* FOR LIFE!

UNTIL THE LAST MOMENT WE MUST STRUGGLE TOGETHER! I NEED YOU!

AND YOU'LL SEE THAT TOGETHER WE'LL SURVIVE.

THIS ALWAYS I TOLD TO HER.

THE GHETTO FINISHED OUT SO LIKE MILOCH SAID. ABOUT TWELVE FROM US RAN INTO HIS BUNKER WITH HIM, HIS WIFE AND HIS THREE-YEARS-OLD BABY BOY.

GUTCHA, YOU'VE GOT TO KEEP THE BABY QUIET!

WAAH! I'M HUNGRY!

WE'LL HAVE TO KEEP HIM UNDER BLANKETS UNTIL HE CALMS DOWN.

HUSH.

IN A BUNKER IN ANOTHER PART FROM THE SHOE SHOP LAY PESACH AND SOME OTHERS.

IT WAS NOTHING TO DO ALL DAY BUT TO LIE AND TO STARVE.

THE WHOLE DAY AND NIGHT ANJA SAT WRITING INTO HER NOTEBOOK.

THERE! I'VE MANAGED TO DIG A SMALL HOLE IN THE STONE WALL.

I CAN SEE SOLDIERS.

ALL AROUND WERE GUARDS TO FIND ANY WHO REMAINED HIDING.

WHAT LITTLE FOOD WE HAD, SOON IT WAS GONE.

OHH... I WISH I HAD SOME BREAD... I WISH I HAD SOME BREAD... I WISH—

QUIET! WE'RE ALL STARVING!

AT NIGHT WE SNEAKED OUT TO LOOK FOR WHAT TO EAT... BUT IT WAS NOTHING TO FIND.

HERE, ANJA— CHEW ON THIS.

YOU FOUND FOOD?

NEVER ANY OF US HAD BEEN SO HUNGRY LIKE THEN.

NO, IT'S ONLY WOOD. BUT CHEWING IT FEELS A LITTLE LIKE EATING FOOD.

AFTER A TIME PESACH CAME OVER TO US FROM HIS BUNKER...

MAYBE YOU FOOLS ARE WILLING TO LIE HERE UNTIL YOU STARVE TO DEATH—BUT NOT ME!...

I'VE CONTACTED ONE OF THE GUARDS.

IT'LL COST A FORTUNE, BUT HE'S AGREED TO LOOK THE OTHER WAY.

OUR GROUP WILL MIX IN WITH THE POLES WHEN THEY WALK PAST SRODULA ON THE WAY TO WORK TOMORROW...
IF YOU WANT TO CHIP IN YOU CAN COME WITH US.

MANY FROM OUR BUNKER SAID YES.

MILOCH AND I, WE SAID NO TO THIS IDEA. WE DIDN'T TRUST TO THE GERMANS.

ONE GUY FROM OUR BUNKER, AVRAM, CAME TO ME.

HE SAID, "TELL ME WHEN *YOU* WILL GO OUT, VLADEK. *THEN* I'LL KNOW IT'S SAFE."

HE AND HIS GIRLFRIEND WANTED TO *PAY* ME TO ADVISE.

THEY HAD STILL 2 WATCHES AND SOME DIAMOND RINGS. I DIDN'T WANT TO TAKE. THEY *NEEDED* THESE TO LIVE.

SO I TOOK ONLY THE SMALL WATCH.

THE NEXT MORNING, VERY EARLY, THE GROUP WALKED OUT.

I STOOD, SECRET, BEHIND A CORNER. I HEARD LOUD SHOOTING, AND I DIDN'T GO TO SEE WHAT HAPPENED...

THEY GAVE OVER THE MONEY AND WENT PAST THE GUARD.

TAKKA TAKKA TAKKA

I ONLY RAN VERY FAST BACK TO OUR BUNKER.

ONLY A FEW OF US REMAINED.

THERE HAVEN'T BEEN ANY LIGHTS ON IN THE GUARD-HOUSE FOR TWO NIGHTS... I THINK IT'S SAFE.

A LITTLE BEFORE DAWN WE WENT OUT FROM SRODULA...

THEY'RE ALL GONE!

WHEW

THE GHETTO IS EMPTY!

AHEAD OF TIME WE ORGANIZED OUR-SELVES GOOD CLOTHES AND I.D. PAPERS.

WE MIXED WITH THE POLES GOING TO WORK.

WE'LL BE HIDING AT THIS AD-DRESS. WHEN YOU FIND A SAFE PLACE, TRY TO CONTACT US, VLADEK.

GOOD LUCK, MILOCH.

WE WENT ALL IN DIF-FERENT DIRECTIONS.

THAT GUY, AVRAM, HIS WOMAN HAD FRIENDS TO KEEP THEM.

AND THE FRIENDS KEPT THEM... UNTIL AVRAM'S MONEY FINISHED. THEN THEY WERE REPORTED.

ANJA AND I DIDN'T HAVE WHERE TO GO.

WE WALKED IN THE DIRECTION OF SOSNOWIEC - BUT **WHERE TO GO?!**

IT WAS **NOWHERE** WE HAD TO HIDE.

CAN I HELP YOU, MR. SPIEGELMAN?

YES, I HAVE HERE MY SON, ARTIE. I WANT TO SIGN HIM A KEY. SO HE CAN GO ALSO TO MY SAFETY BOX.

IN CASE ANYTHING BAD HAPPENS TO ME YOU MUST RUN *RIGHT AWAY* OVER HERE.

THEREFORE I ARRANGED FOR YOU THIS KEY.

TAKE EVERYTHING OUT FROM THE SAFE. OTHERWISE IT CAN GO ONLY TO TAXES. OR *MALA* WILL GRAB IT.

PLEASE, POP...

TALKING ABOUT YOUR ESTATE JUST MAKES ME UNCOMFORTABLE.

YOU'RE NOW OLD ENOUGH SO WE MUST THINK OF THESE THINGS.

WHY DON'T YOU JUST ENJOY YOUR SAVINGS WHILE YOU STILL CAN?

I'LL KEEP IN MY DESK YOUR COPY OF THE KEY. YOU ONLY WOULD LOSE IT!

LOOK, YOU SEE WHAT I HAVE HERE? THIS CIGARETTE CASE AND THE LADY'S POWDER CASE—IT'S 14 KARATS GOLD.

UH HUH

THESE THINGS I HAD WITH ME *THEN*—IN SRODULA, IN THE CHANDELIER BUNKER.

*REALLY?* HOW CAN YOU POSSIBLY STILL HAVE THEM?

WHEN THE GESTAPO FOUND US I DROPPED *QUICK* A FEW THINGS INTO THE CHIMNEY... IF THEY FOUND THE REST OF MY JEWELS, AT LEAST *THESE* MIGHT REMAIN.

AFTER I CAME OUT FROM THE CAMPS IN 1945 I SNEAKED BACK TO SRODULA AND—AT NIGHT, WHILE THE PEOPLE INSIDE SLEPT—I DIGGED THESE THINGS OUT FROM THE BOTTOM OF THE CHIMNEY.

GOSH.

YOU SEE THIS DIAMOND? THIS I GAVE TO ANJA WHEN FIRST WE CAME TO THE U.S.

EVEN WHEN YOU WERE A LITTLE BOY, ANJA WANTED THAT THIS RING SHOULD BE FOR YOUR WIFE.

BUT IF I GIVE IT TO YOU, MALA WILL DRIVE ME CRAZY. SHE WANTS EVERYTHING ONLY FOR HER.

SHE WANTS THAT I GIVE NOTHING FOR MY BROTHER IN ISRAEL, AND NOTHING FOR YOU—THREE TIMES ALREADY SHE MADE ME CHANGE OVER MY WILL.

C'MON— MALA'S OKAY!

YOU ONLY CAN'T KNOW! EVEN RIGHT AFTER MY LAST HEART ATTACK, WHEN STILL I WAS IN BED, SHE STARTED AGAIN ABOUT CHANGING THE WILL!

I SAID, "MALA, YOU SEE HOW SICK I AM. LET ME A LITTLE BIT HAVE SOME PEACE. WHAT YOU WANT FROM ME?"

AND SHE SCREAMED, "I WANT THE MONEY! THE MONEY, THE MONEY!"

WHY, ARTIE? WHY I EVER REMARRIED?

OY, ANJA! ANJA! ANJA!

EASY, POP... LET'S GO HOME.

# CHAPTER SIX

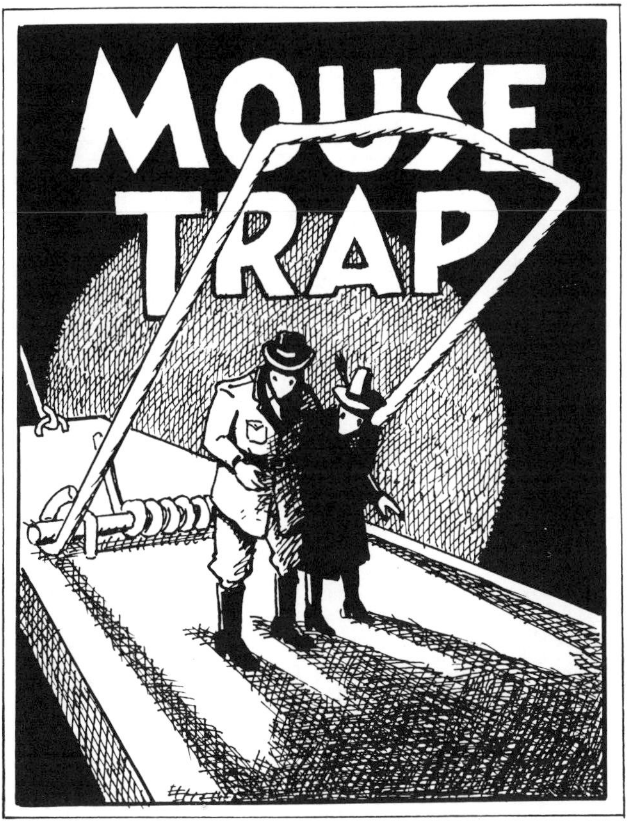
MOUSE
TRAP

Another visit...

ANYBODY HOME?
THE DOOR WASN'T
LOCKED, SO I ...

HUH? MALA?
WERE YOU
CRYING?

NO. SNK
I DON'T KNOW.

I TELL YOU,
I'M AT MY
WITS' END!

WHAT
NOW?

YOUR FATHER! HE TREATS ME
AS IF I WERE JUST A MAID
OR HIS NURSE ... *WORSE!*

AT LEAST A MAID HAS SOME
DAYS OFF AND GETS PAID!

HE ONLY GIVES ME $50⁰⁰ A MONTH.
WHEN I NEED A PAIR OF STOCKINGS
I HAVE TO USE MY OWN SAVINGS!

WELL...
HE HASN'T
CHANGED...

WHENEVER I NEEDED SCHOOL SUPPLIES
OR NEW CLOTHES MOM WOULD HAVE
TO PLEAD AND ARGUE FOR *WEEKS* BE-
FORE HE'D COUGH UP ANY DOUGH!

WHEN *I* TRY TO ARGUE WITH HIM
HE MOANS LIKE HE'S GOING TO
HAVE ANOTHER HEART ATTACK.

I CAN'T BE SURE IF HE'S
FAKING, SO I HAVE TO STOP!

I FEEL LIKE
I'M IN PRISON!

I FEEL LIKE I'M
GOING TO *BURST!*

I'M GONNA GET SOME JUICE. WANT SOME?

NO. I'LL TELL YOU SOMETHING—WHEN WE FIRST GOT MARRIED, I NEEDED CLOTHES...

IT WAS A YEAR AND A HALF AFTER ANJA DIED. HE TOOK ME TO HER CLOSET, AND SAID: "ALL THESE ARE FOR YOU!"

I SAID I WOULDN'T *TOUCH* HER THINGS!

..MY GOD, HOW THAT MAN CARRIED ON! I SWEAR, SOMETIMES I THINK HE MARRIED ME BECAUSE I'M THE SAME SIZE AS ANJA!

HE'S ALWAYS BEEN -UH- PRAGMATIC.

PRAGMATIC? **CHEAP!!** IT CAUSES HIM PHYSICAL PAIN TO PART WITH EVEN A NICKEL!

UH-HUH

I USED TO THINK THE **WAR** MADE HIM THAT WAY...

FAH! I WENT THROUGH THE CAMPS...

ALL OUR FRIENDS WENT THROUGH THE CAMPS. **NOBODY** IS LIKE HIM!

MM..

...IT'S SOMETHING THAT WORRIES ME ABOUT THE BOOK I'M DOING ABOUT HIM...

IN SOME WAYS HE'S JUST LIKE THE RACIST CARICATURE OF THE MISERLY OLD JEW.

HAH! YOU CAN SAY *THAT* AGAIN!

I MEAN, I'M JUST TRYING TO PORTRAY MY FATHER **ACCURATELY!**....

EVEN FOR *HIMSELF* HE WON'T SPEND ANY MONEY...

HE HAS HUNDREDS OF THOUSANDS OF DOLLARS IN THE BANK, AND HE LIVES LIKE A PAUPER! ...

**LOOK!** HE GRABS PAPER TOWELS FROM REST ROOMS SO HE WON'T HAVE TO BUY NAPKINS OR TISSUES!

I WISH I GOT **MOM'S** STORY WHILE SHE WAS ALIVE. SHE WAS MORE *SENSITIVE*...

IT WOULD GIVE THE BOOK SOME BALANCE.

YOUR MOTHER!...

...I JUST DON'T KNOW HOW SHE COULD STAND LIVING WITH HIM...

...I DON'T KNOW HOW *I* CAN STAND IT!

SO..HI, "KIDS."...

I DIDN'T KNOW YOU ARE UPSTAIRS HERE. I WAS WATERING DOWNSTAIRS THE GARDEN.

MALA AND I WERE JUST TALKING ABOUT MY BOOK...

I'VE ALREADY STARTED TO SKETCH OUT SOME PARTS.

I'LL SHOW YOU...

...SEE, HERE ARE THE BLACK MARKET JEWS THEY HANGED IN SOSNOWIEC...

ACH.

AND HERE'S **YOU**, SAYING: "ACH. WHEN I THINK OF THEM, IT STILL MAKES ME CRY!"

YES. **STILL** IT MAKES ME CRY!

IT'S AN IMPORTANT BOOK. PEOPLE WHO DON'T USUALLY READ SUCH STORIES WILL BE INTERESTED.

YES. I DON'T READ **EVER** SUCH COMICS, AND EVEN **I** AM INTERESTED.

OF COURSE **YOU** ARE INTERESTED. IT'S YOUR STORY!

YES. I KNOW ALREADY MY STORY BY **HEART**, AND EVEN **I** AM INTERESTED!

IT SHOULD BE VERY SUCCESSFUL.

YAH. SOMEDAY YOU'LL BE **FAMOUS**, LIKE ...WHAT'S-HIS-NAME?

HUH? "FAMOUS LIKE WHAT'S-HIS-NAME?!"

YOU KNOW... THE BIG-SHOT CARTOONIST...

WHAT CARTOONIST COULD **YOU** KNOW? ...WALT DISNEY??

**YAH! WALT DISNEY!**

WAIT! WHERE DO YOU GO, ARTIE?

...TO GET A PENCIL... I'VE JUST **GOTTA** WRITE THIS CONVERSATION DOWN BEFORE I FORGET IT!

COME. WE'LL ALL OF US GO TO THE GARDEN... YOU'LL SEE HOW NICE IT LOOKS, THE BUSHES.

YOU GO! I'VE GOT TO GET READY...

...I HAVE AN APPOINTMENT AT THE HAIRDRESSER'S.

AGAIN TO THE HAIRDRESSER? ONLY A WEEK AGO YOU WENT!

SHE SEES MORE OFTEN THE HAIRDRESSER THAN SHE SEES ME!

YOU *SEE* HOW IT IS? ANY TIME I WANT TO GO OUT FOR A FEW MINUTES HE TRIES TO MAKE ME FEEL **GUILTY**!

I'M SUPPOSED TO BE AT HIS CONSTANT BECK AND CALL!

WHAT I SAID THAT'S SO TERRIBLE? BELIEVE ME, YOU'D HAVE MORE FRESH AIR FROM THE GARDEN THAN FROM A **HUNDRED** HAIRDRESSERS!

OI, VLADEK. STOP IT!

YOU SEE HOW SHE IS? WHAT HAVE I TO DO WITH HER?

C'MON, POP. LET'S GO SIT IN THE GARDEN.

IF I SAY ONLY ONE WORD TO HER, SHE MAKES RIGHT AWAY AN ARGUMENT!

SHE SAYS SHE WANTS TO **LEAVE** ME! I TELL TO HER: "SO? HERE IS THE DOOR. BUT, REMEMBER, IT'S ONLY ONE WAY... IF YOU GO OUT, YOU CAN'T COME BACK!"

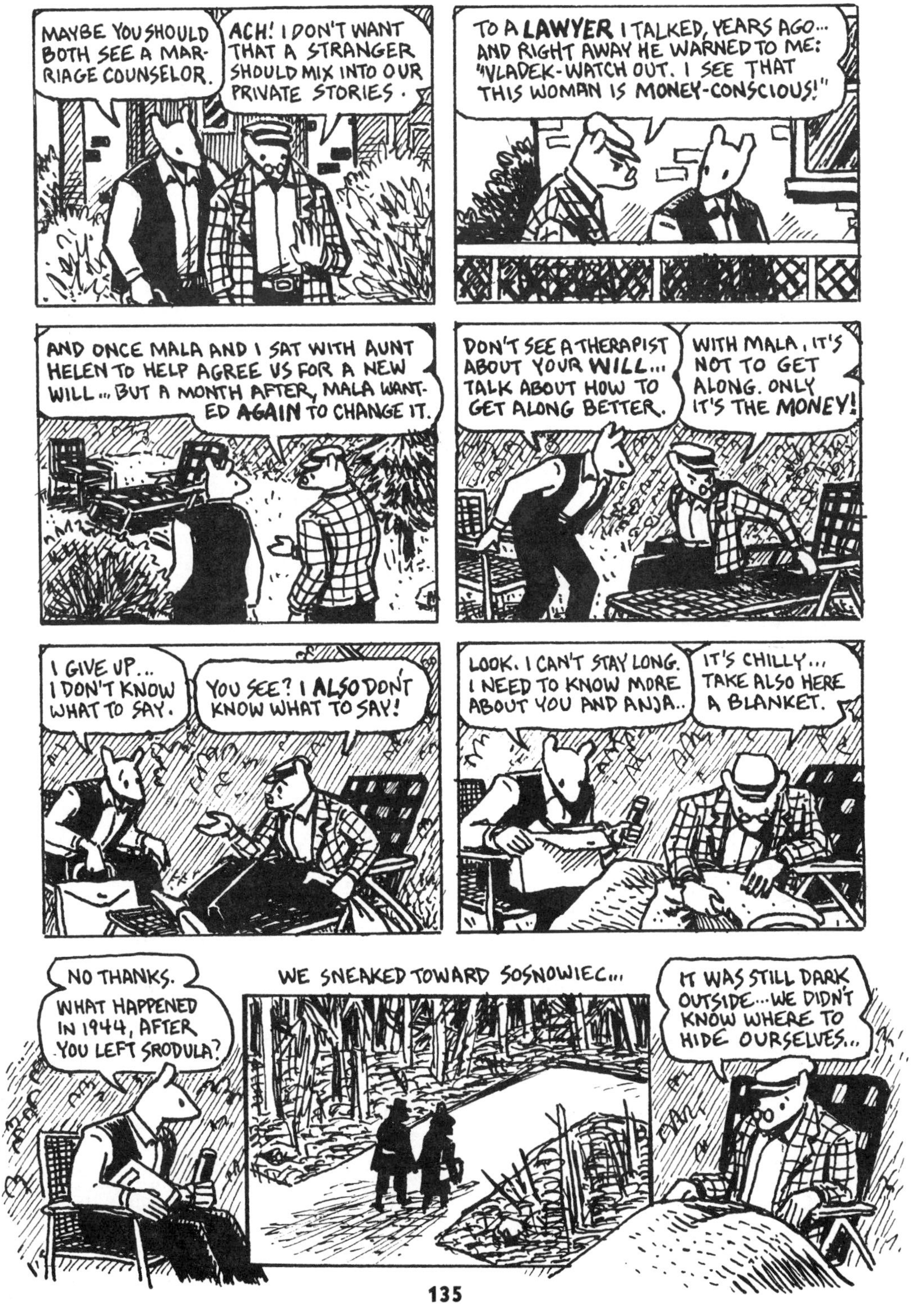
MAYBE YOU SHOULD BOTH SEE A MARRIAGE COUNSELOR.
ACH! I DON'T WANT THAT A STRANGER SHOULD MIX INTO OUR PRIVATE STORIES.
TO A LAWYER I TALKED, YEARS AGO... AND RIGHT AWAY HE WARNED TO ME: "VLADEK-WATCH OUT. I SEE THAT THIS WOMAN IS MONEY-CONSCIOUS!"
AND ONCE MALA AND I SAT WITH AUNT HELEN TO HELP AGREE US FOR A NEW WILL... BUT A MONTH AFTER, MALA WANTED AGAIN TO CHANGE IT.
DON'T SEE A THERAPIST ABOUT YOUR WILL... TALK ABOUT HOW TO GET ALONG BETTER.
WITH MALA, IT'S NOT TO GET ALONG. ONLY IT'S THE MONEY!
I GIVE UP... I DON'T KNOW WHAT TO SAY.
YOU SEE? I ALSO DON'T KNOW WHAT TO SAY!
LOOK. I CAN'T STAY LONG. I NEED TO KNOW MORE ABOUT YOU AND ANJA..
IT'S CHILLY... TAKE ALSO HERE A BLANKET.
NO THANKS.
WHAT HAPPENED IN 1944, AFTER YOU LEFT SRODULA?
WE SNEAKED TOWARD SOSNOWIEC...
IT WAS STILL DARK OUTSIDE... WE DIDN'T KNOW WHERE TO HIDE OURSELVES...

JANINA LIVES OVER THERE.

RICHIEU'S GOVERNESS ALWAYS OFFERED SHE WOULD HELP US.

WE CAME TO HER HOUSE NEAR TOWN...

OPEN UP, JANINA! QUICK!

W-WHO'S THERE?

MY GOD! IT'S THE SPIEGELMANS!

YOU'LL BRING TROUBLE! GO AWAY! *QUICKLY!*

SLAM

I'M FRIGHTENED, VLADEK.

MAYBE WE SHOULD TRY MY FATHER'S OLD HOUSE. THE JANITOR HAS KNOWN OUR FAMILY FOR YEARS.

LET'S TRY. WE'VE **GOT** TO GET OFF THE STREETS BEFORE DAWN!

I WAS A LITTLE SAFE. I HAD A COAT AND BOOTS, SO LIKE A GESTAPO WORE WHEN HE WAS NOT IN SERVICE. BUT **ANJA**—HER APPEARANCE—YOU COULD SEE MORE **EASY** SHE WAS JEWISH. I WAS AFRAID FOR HER.

WAKE UP, MR. LUKOWSKI. LET US IN. *PLEASE!!*

HUH? W-WHO IS IT?

ANJA! ANJA ZYLBERBERG!

WHAT ARE YOU DOING HERE, CHILD? IT ISN'T SAFE! WAIT— I'LL UNLOCK THE GATE.

136

GO THROUGH THE COURTYARD TO THE SHED IN THE BACK. I'LL BRING YOU SOME FOOD.

THANK GOD THERE ARE STILL SOME KIND PEOPLE LEFT. I THOUGHT—

A JEWESS!

THERE'S A JEWESS IN THE COURTYARD! POLICE!

HURRY!

AN OLD WITCH RECOGNIZED ANJA FROM HER WINDOW.

WE RAN FAST TO THE SHED AND HID IN THE STRAW.

IT'S OKAY FOR NOW...

I DON'T THINK ANYONE HEARD HER... SHE'S A LITTLE SENILE ANYWAY.

BUT YOU MUST LOOK FOR A BETTER PLACE TO STAY. SOMEONE HERE IS BOUND TO RECOGNIZE YOU!

IT'S ALMOST MORNING. WAIT HERE. I'M GOING OUT TO SCOUT AROUND.

B-BE CAREFUL.

I WALKED, BUT I DIDN'T KNOW WHERE TO GO.

CLIK CLIK

AND I HEARD SOON IT WAS SOME-BODY FOLLOWING BEHIND ME.

I WALKED SLOW...

CLIK CLIK

BEHIND ME ALSO WALKED SLOW.

IF I WALKED *FAST*...

CLIK

BEHIND ME ALSO WALKED FAST.

WE WERE ALONE. HE SPOKE...

AMCHA?

IN HEBREW HE SAID TO ME, "OUR NATION?"

HAD I TO ANSWER HIM, OR NO?

A-AMCHA.

I *THOUGHT* YOU WERE A JEW...

...I'M JEWISH TOO! THERE ARE VERY FEW OF US LEFT...

...MY WIFE AND I HAVE BEEN HIDING IN SOSNOWIEC FOR OVER A YEAR.

I'M WITH MY WIFE TOO. WE'RE HUNGRY AND WE NEED A PLACE TO HIDE!

GO TO THE BLACK MARKET ON DE-KERTA STREET, NUMBER 8.

SO I LEFT HIM AND WENT RIGHT AWAY TO DEKERTA 8. THERE IT WAS A BIG COURTYARD...

?

ALL AROUND I LOOKED, BUT IT WAS NOBODY.

PSSST!

!

WANNA BUY SOME FOOD WITHOUT COUPONS, MISTER?

SHE SHOWED TO ME SAUSAGES, EGGS, CHEESE ...THINGS I ONLY WAS ABLE TO *DREAM* ABOUT.

I BOUGHT AND WENT QUICK BACK TO ANJA.

GOOD MORNING.

VLADEK! YOU WERE GONE SO LONG.

I HAD TO GET BREAKFAST!... WANT SOME SAUSAGES? ...OR EGGS?..OR WOULD YOU PREFER CHOCOLATE?

WHAT?

IT'S A **MIRACLE!** HOW DID YOU MANAGE IT?

I'M A MAGICIAN! HAVE SOME MILK.

I WENT AGAIN BACK TO DEKERTA. THERE I COULD CHANGE JEWELRY FOR MARKS—AND MARKS FOR FOOD, OR A PLACE TO STAY.

THIS TIME IT WAS MORE PEOPLE...THERE EVEN, I SAW SOME JEWISH BOYS I KNEW FROM BEFORE THE WAR.

VLADEK SPIEGELMAN?! I HARDLY RECOGNIZED YOU. SO YOU'RE STILL ALIVE, EH?

LEO? YES. I'M WITH ANJA.

WE NEED A HIDING PLACE..

HOW ABOUT MRS. KAWKA?

SHE HAS A SMALL FARM ON THE OUTSKIRTS OF TOWN..

SHE MIGHT TAKE YOU IN, IF YOU CAN PAY.

IT WAS NOT SO FAR TO GO TO KAWKA'S FARM...

ALRIGHT THEN, MR. SPIEGELMAN. YOU AND YOUR WIFE CAN STAY IN MY BARN.

WE'LL COME LATE TONIGHT.

BUT, REMEMBER-IF YOU'RE FOUND THERE, I DON'T KNOW YOU! ... YOU MUST SAY THAT THE BARN DOOR WAS OPEN AND YOU JUST SNEAKED IN.

DON'T WORRY...WE WON'T BETRAY YOU!

IT'S ALMOST DAWN-WHEN MRS. KAWKA COMES TO MILK HER COW, SHE'LL BRING YOU SOME COFFEE.

WHERE ARE YOU GOING?

TO DEKERTA.

AND SO WE CAME THERE TO LIVE WITH KAWKA'S COW.

DON'T LEAVE ME ALONE AGAIN. I'M **TERRIFIED** WHILE YOU'RE GONE.

DON'T WORRY, ANJA. I'LL BE SAFE. IF I DIDN'T GO OUT WE WOULDN'T HAVE **FOOD**...WE WOULDN'T HAVE **THIS PLACE**!...

AND WE'VE **GOT** TO FIND A WARMER PLACE FOR THE WINTER...AWAY FROM SOSNOWIEC IF POSSIBLE...

I-I'LL BE OKAY. COME BACK QUICK.

I TRAVELED OFTEN WITH THE STREETCAR TO TOWN.

IT WAS TWO CARS. ONE WAS ONLY GERMANS AND OFFICIALS. THE SECOND, IT WAS ONLY THE POLES.

ALWAYS I WENT STRAIGHT IN THE **OFFICIAL** CAR...

HEIL HITLER.

THE GERMANS PAID NO ATTENTION OF ME.... IN THE **PO-LISH** CAR THEY COULD **SMELL** IF A POLISH JEW CAME IN.

AT THE BLACK MARKET I SAW SEVERAL TIMES A NICE WOMAN, WHAT I MADE A LITTLE FRIENDS WITH HER...

GOOD MORNING, MR. SPIEGELMAN.

HOW DO YOU DO, MRS. MOTONOWA! WHAT DO YOU HAVE IN YOUR BASKET TODAY?

HOW ABOUT A LOAF OF FRESH BREAD?

FINE, FINE,

OH. I'M SORRY. I DON'T HAVE ANY CHANGE.

IT'S OKAY... KEEP IT FOR YOUR LITTLE BOY.

ARE YOU AND YOUR WIFE STILL LIVING IN A BARN?

WE HAVEN'T FOUND ANYTHING BETTER.

I'VE BEEN THINKING ABOUT IT... WHY DON'T YOU BOTH MOVE IN WITH MY SON AND ME?

WHAT ABOUT YOUR HUSBAND?

HE WORKS IN GERMANY, AND ONLY COMES HOME FOR 10 DAYS EVERY 3 MONTHS... I'LL KEEP YOU HIDDEN IN THE CELLAR WHEN HE'S AROUND.

IT SOUNDS GOOD TO ME, BUT IT'S OVER 20 KILOMETERS TO YOUR HOUSE IN SZOPIENICE. MY WIFE WILL BE AFRAID TO GO!

DON'T WORRY. I'LL ESCORT YOU!

THE NEXT EVENING SHE CAME WITH HER 7-YEARS-OLD BOY TO KAWKA'S FARMHOUSE...

I WALKED WITH MOTONOWA AS IF *SHE* WAS MY WIFE.

AND ANJA, LIKE A GOVERNESS, WENT WITH THE LITTLE BOY BEHIND. AND NOBODY EVEN *LOOKED* ON US.

WE HAD HERE A LITTLE COMFORTABLE... WE HAD WHERE TO SIT.

REMEMBER, LITTLE ONE — NEVER TELL **ANYBODY** THERE ARE JEWS HERE. THEY'LL SHOOT US ALL!

YES, AUNT ANJA.

THE LITTLE BOY WAS VERY SMART AND HE LOVED VERY MUCH ANJA.

YOU HAD TO **PAY** MRS. MOTONOWA TO KEEP YOU, RIGHT?

OF COURSE I PAID... AND **WELL** I PAID.

...WHAT YOU THINK? SOMEONE WILL RISK THEIR LIFE FOR NOTHING?

...I PAID ALSO FOR THE **FOOD** WHAT SHE GAVE TO US FROM HER SMUGGLING BUSINESS.

BUT, ONE TIME I MISSED A FEW COINS TO THE BREAD...

I'LL PAY YOU THE REST TOMORROW, AFTER I GO OUT AND CASH SOME VALUABLES.

SORRY... I WASN'T ABLE TO **FIND** ANY BREAD TODAY.

**ALWAYS** SHE GOT BREAD, SO I DIDN'T BELIEVE... BUT, STILL, SHE WAS A GOOD WOMAN.

IN HIS SCHOOL THE BOY WAS VERY BAD IN GERMAN. SO ANJA TUTORED TO HIM.

ICH BIN... DU BIST... ER IST...

SHE KNEW GERMAN LIKE AN EXPERT.

AND SOON HE CAME OUT WITH **VERY** GOOD GRADES.

MY TEACHER ASKED ME HOW I IMPROVED SO MUCH...

SO I TOLD HIM MY **MOTHER** WAS HELPING ME.

WHEW

HE WAS REALLY A CLEVER BOY.

BUT IT WAS A FEW THINGS HERE NOT SO GOOD... HER HOME WAS VERY SMALL AND IT WAS ON THE GROUND FLOOR...

BE SURE TO KEEP AWAY FROM THE WINDOW — YOU MIGHT BE SEEN!

NOK NOK

ONE MINUTE! (QUICK-GET IN THE CLOSET!)

IF SOMEBODY CAME, WE HAD FAST TO HIDE,

A LETTER FROM YOUR HUSBAND, MRS. MOTONOWA.

THANKS.

BUT I HAD SOMETHING ALLERGIC IN THE CLOSET...

AAH-

OR MAYBE IT WAS A COLD-I CAN'T REMEMBER...

-CHMF

BUT ALWAYS I HAD TO SNEEZE.

STILL, EVERYTHING HERE WAS FINE, UNTIL ONE SATURDAY MOTONOWA RAN VERY EARLY BACK FROM HER BLACK MARKET WORK...

THIS IS TERRIBLE!

THE GESTAPO JUST SEARCHED ME...THEY TOOK MY GOODS!

THEY MAY COME SEARCH HERE ANY MINUTE! YOU'VE GOT TO LEAVE!

WHAT?

BUT WHERE CAN WE GO?

I DON'T KNOW. BUT YOU MUST GET OUT **NOW!**

OH MY GOD...THIS IS THE END!

ANJA STARTED TO CRY... BUT WE HAD NOT A CHOICE.

WE'LL WALK TOWARD SOS-NOWIEC – AT LEAST WE'LL KNOW OUR WAY AROUND.

ANJA WAS SO AFRAID SHE WAS SHAKING.

STAY CALM – WALK AS IF WE'RE JUST STROLLING ... AND SPEAK GERMAN.

FOR HOURS WE WALKED.

B-BESUCHEN WIR DOCH FRAU KAWKA.

GUTE IDEE.

VLADEK-WE'RE BEING FOLLOWED.

RELAX

BUT IF WE TURNED A COR-NER, THEY ALSO TURNED.

ES IST KALT.

JA. JA.

OF COURSE I WAS RIGHT – THEY DIDN'T MEAN ANYTHING ON US.

WOOSH

THEY JUST WERE WALKING.

STAYING ON THE STREET ALL NIGHT IS TOO DANGEROUS... MAYBE WE CAN HIDE IN THAT CONSTRUCTION SITE.

GOOD-I'M EXHAUSTED.

HERE WAS A FOUNDATION MADE VERY DEEP DOWN IN THE GROUND..

BE CAREFUL!

I JUMPED FIRST IN, AND I PULLED OVER BRICKS FOR ANJA TO STEP DOWN.

AND HERE WE WAITED A COLD FEW HOURS FOR THE DAY.

144

IT STARTED TO BE LIGHT...

COME. WE WON'T BE NOTICED IF WE MIX WITH PEOPLE OUT ON THE STREET.

I'M SO TIRED AND COLD...

WE CAN REST NOW.

WE CAME FINALLY AGAIN TO THIS PLACE WITH THE COW AND WENT INSIDE.

LATER, KAWKA CAME IN...

W-WHO'S IN HERE?

THE SPIEGEL-MANS... WE HAD NOWHERE ELSE TO GO.

WELL... I GUESS YOU CAN STAY. BUT, REMEMBER: I DON'T KNOW YOU'RE HERE!

WHY, MRS. SPIEGELMAN, YOU'RE SHIVERING!

YOU CAN COME INTO MY HOUSE FOR AN HOUR OR SO, 'TIL YOU WARM UP.

SHE TOOK ANJA INSIDE AND BROUGHT TO ME SOME FOOD...IN THOSE DAYS I WAS SO STRONG I COULD SIT EVEN IN THE SNOW ALL NIGHT...

THINGS CAN'T BE THIS BAD EVERYWHERE! I'D GIVE ANYTHING TO GET OUT OF POLAND!

YOU KNOW, BEFORE I TOOK YOU IN, I HAD A YOUNG MAN AND HIS SON HERE...

TWO PEOPLE I KNOW SMUG-GLED THEM INTO HUNGARY. I HEARD HE AND HIS BOY WERE DOING WELL THERE.

HUNGARY! REALLY?! I'D LIKE TO MEET THOSE SMUGGLERS!

SHE TOLD ME THESE TWO ACQUAINTANCES VISITED OFTEN TO HER ON THURS-DAY EVENINGS.... TODAY WAS MAYBE A MONDAY...

I DON'T GET IT... WASN'T HUNGARY AS DANGEROUS AS POLAND?

NO. FOR A LONGER TIME IT WAS *BETTER* THERE IN HUNGARY FOR THE JEWS... BUT THEN, NEAR THE VERY FINISH OF THE WAR, THEY ALL GOT PUT *ALSO* TO AUSCHWITZ.

I WAS THERE, AND I SAW IT. THOUSANDS- HUNDREDS OF THOUSANDS OF JEWS FROM HUNGARY...

SO MANY, IT WASN'T EVEN ROOM ENOUGH TO BURY THEM ALL IN THE OVENS.

BUT AT THAT TIME, WHEN I WAS THERE WITH KAWKA, WE COULDN'T *KNOW* THEN.

SO.... I WENT NEXT DAY TO DEKERTA STREET TO BUY FOOD...

OH GOD! OH GOD! MR. SPIEGELMAN, YOU'RE ALIVE! I'M SO GLAD TO SEE YOU!

MRS. MOTO-NOWA!

I WANTED TO FIND A NEW CONNECTION TO HIDE US. BUT *REALLY* I DIDN'T THINK TO FIND AGAIN *HER.*

PRAISE MARY, YOU'RE SAFE! I COULDN'T *SLEEP,* I FELT SO GUILTY ABOUT CHASING YOU AND YOUR WIFE OUT.

THE GESTAPO NEVER EVEN CAME TO MY HOUSE. I JUST PANICKED FOR NOTHING.

PLEASE COME BACK AGAIN.

ANJA WAS GLAD OF GOING BACK. AND MOTONOWA ALSO... ALWAYS I PAID HER NICELY.

AND THAT SAME NIGHT WE SAID GOODBYE TO KAWKA AND WENT AGAIN TO SZOPIENICE.

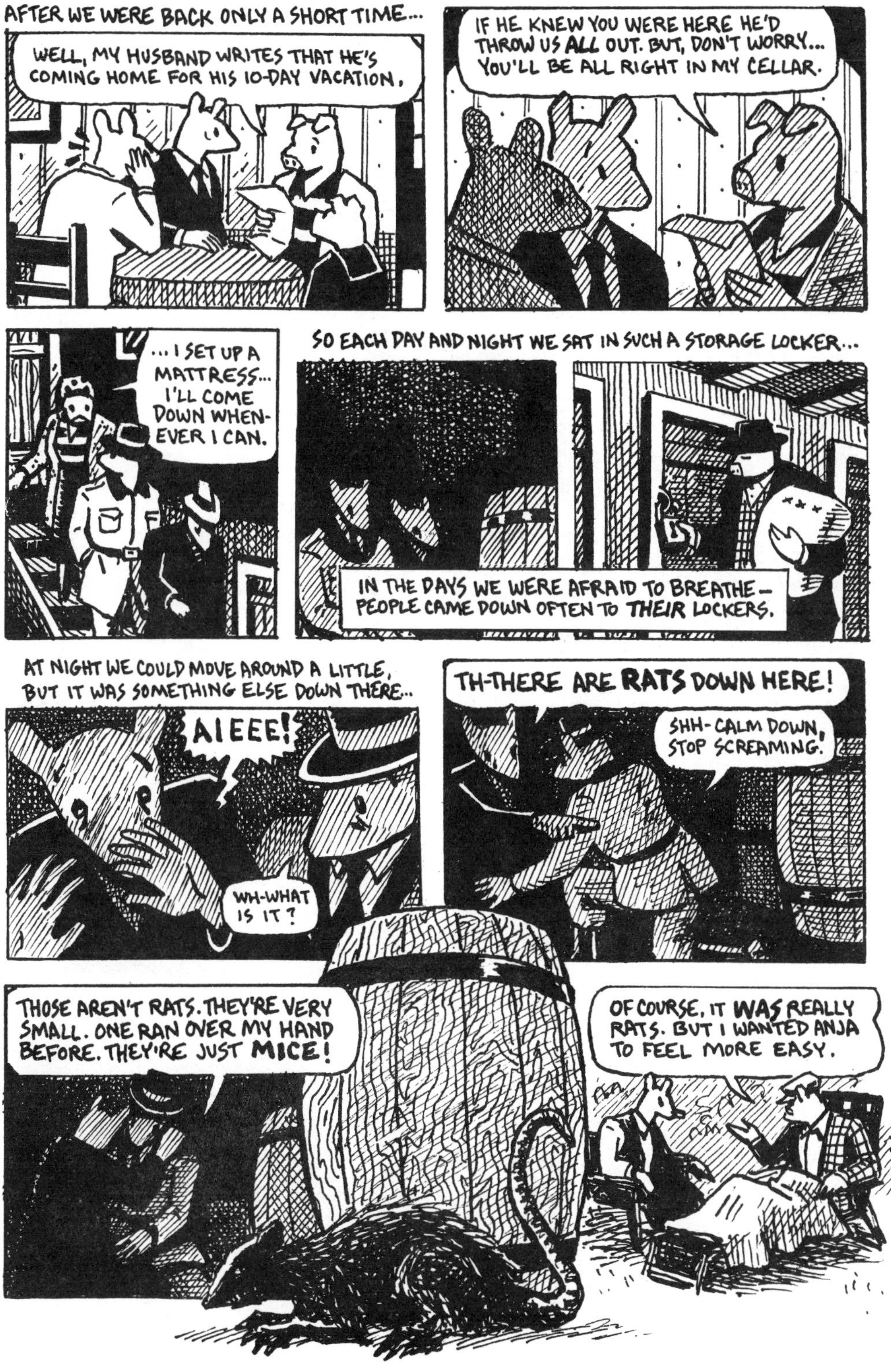
AFTER WE WERE BACK ONLY A SHORT TIME...
WELL, MY HUSBAND WRITES THAT HE'S COMING HOME FOR HIS 10-DAY VACATION.
IF HE KNEW YOU WERE HERE HE'D THROW US ALL OUT. BUT, DON'T WORRY... YOU'LL BE ALL RIGHT IN MY CELLAR.
...I SET UP A MATTRESS... I'LL COME DOWN WHENEVER I CAN.
SO EACH DAY AND NIGHT WE SAT IN SUCH A STORAGE LOCKER...
IN THE DAYS WE WERE AFRAID TO BREATHE— PEOPLE CAME DOWN OFTEN TO THEIR LOCKERS.
AT NIGHT WE COULD MOVE AROUND A LITTLE, BUT IT WAS SOMETHING ELSE DOWN THERE...
AIEEE!
WH-WHAT IS IT?
TH-THERE ARE RATS DOWN HERE!
SHH- CALM DOWN, STOP SCREAMING!
THOSE AREN'T RATS. THEY'RE VERY SMALL. ONE RAN OVER MY HAND BEFORE. THEY'RE JUST MICE!
OF COURSE, IT WAS REALLY RATS. BUT I WANTED ANJA TO FEEL MORE EASY.

BUT, THEN, MOTONOWA STOPPED TO COME DOWN.

IT'S BEEN 3 DAYS SINCE SHE BROUGHT ANY FOOD.

HERE... HAVE ANOTHER CANDY...

I HAD STILL CANDIES I ORGANIZED ON DEKERTA. ONLY **THIS** WE HAD TO EAT.

ALSO, HERE WE HAD NO PLACE WHERE TO WASH, SO ANJA GOT ON ALL HER SKIN A TERRIBLE RASH.

I DON'T KNOW WHAT'S WORSE—THE HUNGER OR THE ITCHING.

DON'T SCRATCH! IT ONLY—SHH!

CLIK

THE DOOR.

I'M SORRY I COULDN'T GET DOWN BEFORE... MY HUSBAND IS GETTING SUSPICIOUS.

HE ASKED WHY I GO TO THE CELLAR SO OFTEN. HE EVEN ASKED IF I WAS HIDING **JEWS** HERE!
...HE WAS **JOKING,** BUT STILL...

ARE YOU ALL RIGHT HERE?

THERE ARE **RATS,** GIANT RATS! THEY'RE HORRIBLE!

WELL—YOU'RE BETTER OFF WITH THE RATS THAN WITH THE GESTAPO...
AT LEAST THE RATS WON'T **KILL** YOU!

MMM...

AND SHE WAS RIGHT. WE WERE HAPPY EVEN TO HAVE **THESE** CONDITIONS.

AFTER THE TEN DAYS HER HUSBAND LEFT, AND SHE TOOK US BACK.

IT'S GOOD TO BE "HOME," EH, VLADEK?

IT'S A LOT NICER THAN THAT CELLAR.

BUT I DIDN'T FEEL SAFE HERE. IT WAS TOO MANY WAYS SOMEBODY COULD FIND US OUT. I WANTED TO GO BETTER TO HUNGARY.

SO, WHEN IT CAME THURSDAY, I WENT IN THE DIRECTION TO TAKE A STREETCAR TO SEE KAWKA IN SOSNOWIEC.

A JEW! A JEW!

LOOK!

I HAD TO PASS WHERE SOME CHILDREN WERE PLAYING.

THEY RAN SCREAMING HOME.

HELP! MOMMY! A JEW!!

A JEW!

QUICK, THE MOTHERS CAME OUTSIDE TO SEE WHAT WAS!

THE MOTHERS ALWAYS TOLD SO: "BE CAREFUL! A JEW WILL CATCH YOU TO A BAG AND EAT YOU!" ... SO THEY TAUGHT TO THEIR CHILDREN.

I APPROACHED OVER TO THEM...

HEIL HITLER.

IF I RAN AWAY THEY, WOULD SEE: "YES, IT IS A JEW HERE."

DON'T BE AFRAID, LITTLE ONES. I'M NOT A JEW. I WON'T HURT YOU.

SORRY, MISTER. YOU KNOW HOW KIDS ARE... HEIL HITLER.

SO I CAME OUT WELL FROM THIS...

BUT THE EXPERIENCE COST ME REALLY A LOT OF HAIRS.

149

WHEN I ARRIVED TO KAWKA, THE TWO SMUGGLERS WERE THERE TOGETHER SITTING IN THE KITCHEN..

PLEASE WAIT IN THE OTHER ROOM. THEY'LL SEE YOU SOON.

MR. MANDELBAUM!

VLADEK SPIEGELMAN!

MANDELBAUM, BEFORE THE WAR OWNED A SWEETS SHOP.

ANJA AND I BOUGHT ALWAYS PASTRIES THERE. HE USED TO BE A VERY RICH MAN IN SOSNOWIEC.

THIS IS MY WIFE...AND YOU KNOW MY NEPHEW..

HELLO, ABRAHAM. WHAT ARE YOU ALL DOING HERE?

BACK WHEN IT WAS THE GHETTO, ABRAHAM WAS A BIG MEMBER OF THE JEWISH COUNCIL.

WE'RE TRYING TO GET OUT OF POLAND—

—TO HUNGARY?! YES. ANJA AND I ARE TRYING TO ARRANGE THAT TOO!

THE SMUGGLERS PROPOSED US HOW THEY WOULD DO.

...AND AT THE BORDER OUR PARTNERS WILL TAKE YOU THROUGH THE MOUNTAINS.

WHEW— IT'S RISKY AND VERY EXPENSIVE!

WE SPOKE YIDDISH SO THE POLES DON'T UNDERSTAND.

NIE, VAS DENKST DIE?

YECH KENN DIE FRAU KAWKA, UBER YECH BIN NISH ZICHER VEGEN DIE ZWEI.

So, what do you think?

I know Mrs. Kawka, but I'm not sure about these two.

HERR MECHTSE! YECH GEI KOIDEM MIT ZEI. AZ ALLES VET ZEIN BESEDER, YECH VIL SCHREIBEN TSE DEYER.

Listen! I'll go first. If everything is okay, I'll write back to you.

THE OTHERS WANT TO THINK ABOUT IT A LITTLE LONGER, BUT I'M READY TO GO NOW.

FINE, FINE.

I AGREED WITH MANDELBAUM TO MEET AGAIN HERE. IF IT CAME A GOOD LETTER, WE'LL GO.

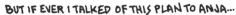

NO, VLADEK! YOU'RE CRAZY! IT'S TOO DANGEROUS!

BUT IF WE HEAR FROM ABRAHAM—

WE'RE SAFE HERE- FORGET ABOUT HUNGARY!

BUT WHAT DO WE DO IF THE GESTAPO COMES TO SEARCH FOR ILLEGAL GOODS? ...WHAT IF A NEIGHBOR NOTICES US THROUGH THE KITCHEN WINDOW?...

I'M NOT GOING!

WHAT IF HER HUSBAND FINDS OUT ABOUT US? EVEN THE BOY COULD LET SOMETHING SLIP! ...THIS WAR COULD LAST ANOTHER 4 OR 5 YEARS. WHAT DO WE DO WHEN OUR MONEY RUNS OUT?

PLEASE!

IN HUNGARY WE COULD BE FREE TO WALK THE STREETS AGAIN, LIKE HUMAN BEINGS... I'VE ALWAYS TAKEN CARE OF YOU- TRUST ME.

I'M SO SCARED. >SOB<

DON'T DO IT, MR. SPIEGELMAN— IT'S JUST NOT SAFE! YOU DON'T KNOW ANYTHING ABOUT THESE SMUGGLERS.

SNF. IT'S LIKE TALKING TO A WALL.

WE WON'T GO UNLESS WE HEAR THAT OUR FRIEND GOT THROUGH.

I'VE HAD AWFUL NIGHTMARES ABOUT YOUR TRIP- PLEASE STAY WITH ME!

SNF

WAIT- NOW WHERE ARE YOU GOING?

-TO VISIT MY COUSIN AND SEE WHERE HE'S HIDING. IF WE DO GO TO HUNGARY, HE MAY BE BETTER OFF HERE WITH YOU!

MILOCH HELPED ME IN SRODULA. MAYBE NOW, IF HE NEEDED, I COULD HELP HIM.

THE JANITOR IN THE HOUSE MILOCH OWNED, SHE HID NOW HIM AND HIS FAMILY; BUT —OH BOY— HE WAS IN A SITUATION WORSE AS I COULD IMAGINE!

I WENT TO THE JANITOR BY TROLLEY

HELLO— I'M MILOCH'S COUSIN, VLADEK.

YES. HE TOLD ME YOU MIGHT COME.

I HAVE SOME COMPANY UPSTAIRS. I CAN'T TAKE YOU TO MILOCH UNTIL THEY LEAVE.

GENTLEMEN. THIS IS MY COUSIN, VLADEK.

HI "CUZ," HAVE A DRINK.

SO WE TALKED, AND THEY BELIEVED I AM HER COUSIN.

WE'RE ALMOST OUT OF VODKA. BRING SOME MORE, MEINKA.

THERE ISN'T ANY.

BAH! SHE'S HIDING HER VODKA!

JUST LIKE SHE'S HIDING JEWS IN HER YARD!

THE JANITOR AND I FROZE OUR BLOOD FROM FEAR...

IF YOU DON'T PUT ANOTHER BOTTLE ON THE TABLE RIGHT AWAY, WE'LL TELL THE GESTAPO ABOUT THE JEWS YOU'RE KEEPING!!

R-RELAX FELLOWS.

HERE'S A FEW MARKS, MEINKA. RUN DOWNSTAIRS AND GET ANOTHER BOTTLE FOR OUR FRIENDS.

'ATTA BOY. HIC.

IN 15 MINUTES SHE CAME WITH A BOTTLE AND THEY WERE HAPPY.

YOU SEE? YOUR COUSIN KNOWS HOW TO ENTERTAIN GUESTS! TO YOUR HEALTH.

WE DRANK AND WE DRANK— ONLY NEAR MIDNIGHT FINALLY THEY WENT HOME.

I THINK IT'S SAFE TO GO DOWN.

ARE YOU -SNF- CARRYING *FOOD* FOR MILOCH?

I FED THEM EARLIER. THIS IS JUST *TRASH*.

THE CONDITIONS HOW MILOCH WAS LIVING-YOU COULDN'T BELIEVE.

...I ALWAYS BRING GARBAGE SO THE NEIGHBORS DON'T GET SUSPICIOUS.

PSST-MILOCH. YOUR COUSIN IS HERE.

?

IN EACH COURTYARD WAS A VERY DEEP HOLE TO THROW IN ALL THE GARBAGE.

INSIDE THIS GARBAGE HOLE WAS HERE SEPARATED A TINY SPACE — MAYBE ONLY 5 FEET BY 6 FEET.

VLADEK! I'M GLAD YOU'RE STILL ALIVE!

MY GOD!

I LOOKED DOWN ONLY FOR A SECOND, BUT IN THERE WAS LIVING MILOCH, HIS WIFE AND THEIR 3-YEARS-OLD BOY.

HOW CAN YOU *LIVE* THERE? YOU MUST BE FREEZING!

WE HAVE NO CHOICE. AT LEAST OUR BUNKKER IS UNDERGROUND..

AND THE DECOMPOSING GARBAGE GIVES SOME HEAT.

BUT PEOPLE *KNOW* YOU'RE IN THERE...

I TOLD HIM MY STORY WITH THESE POLES UPSTAIRS.

WHAT CAN WE DO?

LISTEN-ANJA AND I MAY BE GOING TO HUNGARY!..

I EXPLAINED OUR HIDING PLACE WAS NOT PERFECT, BUT BETTER THAN HIS.

I'LL COME AGAIN WHEN I HAVE MORE NEWS, BUT IT'S VERY LATE NOW — I MUST GET BACK HOME.

AND I WAS LUCKY. NOBODY MADE ME ANY QUESTIONS GOING BACK TO SZOPIENICE.

A FEW DAYS AFTER, I CAME AGAIN TO THE SMUGGLERS. AND MANDELBAUM WAS ALSO THERE.

LOOK, VLADEK—MY NEPHEW IS SAFE! THEY BROUGHT ME A LETTER FROM HIM.

IT WAS IN YIDDISH AND IT WAS SIGNED REALLY BY ABRAHAM. SO WE AGREED RIGHT AWAY TO GO AHEAD.

BUT ANJA JUST DIDN'T WANT WE WOULD GO...

PLEASE, VLADEK, CALL IT OFF!

BUT IT'S ALL ARRANGED. I'VE EVEN GIVEN THEM HALF THEIR MONEY!

NO! NO! NO! IT'S SOME KIND OF TRICK!

BE REASONABLE. I SAW ABRAHAM'S LETTER WITH MY OWN EYES!

WH-WHAT DID IT SAY?

"DEAR AUNT AND UNCLE, EVERYTHING IS WONDERFUL HERE. I ARRIVED SAFELY. I'M FREE AND HAPPY. DON'T LOSE A MINUTE. JOIN ME AS SOON AS YOU CAN. YOUR LOVING NEPHEW, ABRAHAM."

I-I DON'T KNOW...

WE LEAVE THE DAY AFTER TOMORROW FROM THE KATOWICE TRAIN STATION.

AND FINALLY I CONVINCED HER.

SO, I WENT ONE MORE TIME OVER TO MILOCH IN HIS GARBAGE BUNKER AND DIRECTED HIM HOW HE MUST GO TO SZOPIENICE AND HIDE...

AND, YOU KNOW, MILOCH AND HIS WIFE AND BOY, THEY ALL SURVIVED THEMSELVES THE WHOLE WAR... SITTING THERE ... WITH MOTONOWA...

BUT, FOR ANJA AND I, IT WAS FOR US WAITING ANOTHER DESTINY...

WE CAME WITH NO PROBLEM BY TROLLEY CAR TO OUR MEETING POINT WITH THE MANDELBAUMS AND THE SMUGGLERS.

EVERYTHING IS ARRANGED. HERE ARE YOUR TICKETS.

DO YOU HAVE THE REST OF OUR PAYMENT?

YES. OF COURSE. HERE.

WH-WHERE IS YOUR PARTNER GOING?

HE'S PHONING AHEAD TO THE MEN WHO WILL MEET YOU AT THE BORDER. HE'LL JOIN US ON THE TRAIN-DON'T WORRY!

BUT, OF COURSE, WE *DID* WORRY...

SO, ALL OF US TOGETHER STARTED ON OUR JOURNEY...

WE TRAVELED LESS THAN AN HOUR 'TIL WE CAME TO BIELSKO-BIALA. HERE I USED TO HAVE MY FACTORY. AND HERE THE SMUGGLERS DISAPPEARED.

IT WAS A BIG COMMOTION... GESTAPO CAME ON EVERY SIDE

JUDEN RAUS!

HERE THEY ARE!

IN KATOWICE, IT WAS ONLY TO *THEM* THE SMUGGLER PHONED.

THEY MARCHED US THROUGH THE CITY OF BIELSKO. WE PASSED BY THE FACTORY WHAT ONCE I OWNED...

WE PASSED THE MARKET WHERE ALWAYS WE BOUGHT TO EAT, AND PASSED EVEN THE STREET WHERE WE USED TO LIVE, AND WE CAME 'TIL THE PRISON, AND THERE THEY PUT US.

I HAD A SMALL BAG TO TRAVEL. WHEN THEY REGISTERED ME IN, THEY LOOKED OVER EVERYTHING.

WHAT'S THIS? SHOE POLISH??

YES. I LIKE TO KEEP MYSELF NEAT.

WITH A SPOON HE TOOK OUT, LITTLE BY LITTLE, ALL THE POLISH.

WELL, WELL... A GOLD WATCH. ..YOU JEWS *ALWAYS* HAVE GOLD!

WRAPPED IN FOIL, I KEPT IT HIDDEN THERE... IT WAS MY LAST TREASURE.

IT WAS THIS WATCH I GOT FROM FATHER-IN-LAW WHEN FIRST I MARRIED TO ANJA.

WELL, NEVER MIND...THEY TOOK IT AND THREW ME WITH MANDELBAUM INTO A CELL...

WAIT A MINUTE! WHAT EVER HAPPENED TO ABRAHAM?

WHO?

AH, MANDELBAUM'S NEPHEW! YES. HE FINISHED THE SAME AS US TO CONCENTRATION CAMP.

-BUT

YES. I'LL TELL YOU HOW IT WAS WITH HIM- BUT NOW I'M TELLING HERE IN THE PRISON...

HERE WE GOT VERY LITTLE TO EAT—MAYBE SOUP ONE TIME A DAY-AND WE SAT WITH NOTHING TO DO.

WHY DON'T THEY PUT US TO WORK LIKE THE REST OF YOU?

IT MEANS YOU WON'T BE HERE VERY LONG...

...EVERY WEEK OR SO A TRUCK TAKES SOME OF THE PRISONERS AWAY.

EXCUSE ME... DO ANY OF YOU KNOW GERMAN?

MY FAMILY JUST SENT ME A FOOD PARCEL. IF I WRITE BACK THEY'LL SEND ANOTHER, BUT WE'RE ONLY ALLOWED TO WRITE GERMAN.

I KNEW *WELL* TO WRITE GERMAN...SO I WROTE...

IN A SHORT TIME HE GOT AGAIN A PACKAGE...

YOU DID A GREAT JOB! TAKE ANYTHING YOU WANT FOR YOU AND YOUR FRIEND!

IT WAS EGGS THERE....IT WAS EVEN CHOCOLATES. ...I WAS VERY LUCKY TO GET SUCH GOODIES!

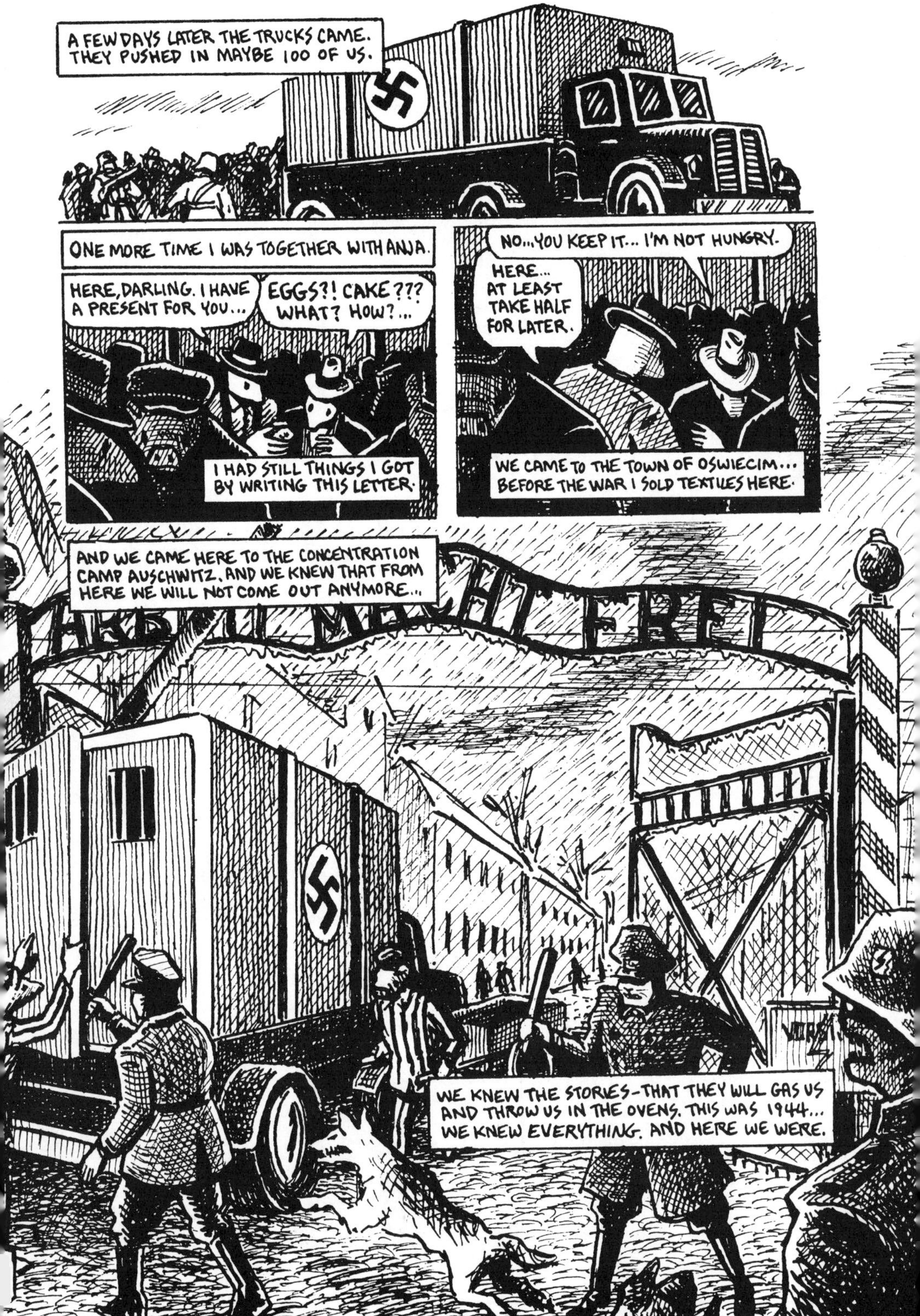

A FEW DAYS LATER THE TRUCKS CAME. THEY PUSHED IN MAYBE 100 OF US.
ONE MORE TIME I WAS TOGETHER WITH ANJA.
HERE, DARLING. I HAVE A PRESENT FOR YOU...
EGGS?! CAKE??? WHAT? HOW?...
I HAD STILL THINGS I GOT BY WRITING THIS LETTER.
NO... YOU KEEP IT... I'M NOT HUNGRY.
HERE... AT LEAST TAKE HALF FOR LATER.
WE CAME TO THE TOWN OF OSWIECIM... BEFORE THE WAR I SOLD TEXTILES HERE.
AND WE CAME HERE TO THE CONCENTRATION CAMP AUSCHWITZ, AND WE KNEW THAT FROM HERE WE WILL NOT COME OUT ANYMORE...
WE KNEW THE STORIES - THAT THEY WILL GAS US AND THROW US IN THE OVENS. THIS WAS 1944... WE KNEW EVERYTHING. AND HERE WE WERE.

MY GOD.

YES. SO IT WAS...

...AND WHEN THEY OPENED THE TRUCK, THEY PUSHED MEN ONE WAY, WOMEN TO THE OTHER WAY...

ANJA AND I WENT EACH IN A DIFFERENT DIRECTION, AND WE COULDN'T KNOW IF EVER WE'LL SEE EACH OTHER ALIVE AGAIN.

THIS IS WHERE MOM'S DIARIES WILL BE *ESPECIALLY* USEFUL. THEY'LL GIVE ME SOME IDEA OF WHAT SHE WENT THROUGH WHILE YOU WERE APART.

I CAN TELL YOU ... SHE WENT THROUGH THE SAME WHAT ME: TERRIBLE!

IT'S GETTING COLD. WHY DON'T WE GO UPSTAIRS AND SEE IF WE CAN FIND HER NOTEBOOKS...

NO... I *LOOKED* ALREADY...

...IT'S JUST NOT TO *FIND* ANYMORE!

WELL... LET'S CHECK OUT THE GARAGE. YOU'VE GOT LOADS OF STUFF IN THERE.

NO. YOU'LL NOT FIND IT. BECAUSE I REMIND TO MYSELF WHAT HAPPENED...

THESE NOTEBOOKS, AND OTHER REALLY NICE THINGS OF MOTHER... ONE TIME I HAD A VERY BAD DAY... AND ALL OF THESE THINGS I *DESTROYED*.

YOU *WHAT?*

AFTER ANJA DIED I HAD TO MAKE AN ORDER WITH EVERYTHING... THESE PAPERS HAD TOO MANY MEMORIES. SO I BURNED THEM.

YOU BURNED THEM?

CHRIST! YOU SAVE TONS OF WORTHLESS SHIT, AND YOU...

YES, IT'S A SHAME! FOR YEARS THEY WERE LAYING THERE AND NOBODY EVEN LOOKED IN.

DID YOU EVER READ ANY OF THEM?... CAN YOU REMEMBER WHAT SHE WROTE?

NO. I LOOKED IN, BUT I DON'T REMEMBER...ONLY I KNOW THAT SHE SAID, "I WISH MY SON, WHEN HE GROWS UP, HE WILL BE INTERESTED BY THIS."

GOD DAMN YOU! YOU-YOU MURDERER! HOW THE HELL COULD YOU DO SUCH A THING!!

ACH

TO YOUR FATHER YOU YELL IN THIS WAY?... EVEN TO YOUR FRIENDS YOU SHOULD NEVER YELL THIS WAY!

BUT, I'M TELLING YOU, AFTER THE TRAGEDY WITH MOTHER, I WAS SO DEPRESSED THEN, I DIDN'T KNOW IF I'M COMING OR I'M GOING!

I'M SORRY. LOOK, POP. IT'S GETTING LATE. I'D BETTER GET HOME...

COME FIRST UPSTAIRS FOR A LITTLE COFFEE.

NO...REALLY. I'D BETTER GET GOING RIGHT AWAY...

SO,..TELEPHONE TO ME,... YOU SHOULD VISIT HERE MORE OFTEN—DON'T BE SUCH A STRANGER!

SURE... YOU BET! SO LONG.

...MURDERER.

159

NEXT:

*Maus: A Survivor's Tale*

Part Two, "From Mauschwitz to the Catskills"

(Winter 1944 to the Present)